FALLEN PEPPERCORNS

Fallen Peppercorns

A Story of Resilience

KEVIN MEEHAN

Isosceles Holdings LLC

Foreword

The idea of writing this book has been hibernating within me for more than twenty years. After discarding the needless embarrassment and shame of the incidents I went through, the primary motivation to bring my story out into the open for the public to see was due to the vast number of people I have witnessed who have either had or are having a difficult time progressing in their lives because of past trauma in their lives. Enduring these experiences in either their youth or perhaps recently often provokes challenges in resolving such issues which can hinder their lives in a negative way. Many times the idea that these experiences are unique to an individual may invite a degree of isolation into their lives until perhaps they see that it may not be that unusual after all.

All of this would never have come to fruition if I had allowed the traumatic events, which are made public for the first time in this book, to hinder the motivation granted to me by my actions of self-love and acceptance. The realization that I am no more or less special than my fellow human and yet able to develop a fulfilling life that encompasses developing a successful career in many fields which helps many others, is one of the deep-seated meanings held within the written words on these pages. These very words hold the hopes of allowing the reader to capture the essence of their true spirit and to relinquish itself from the traumatic events of their past, understanding that these very events were experiences which are not capable of diminishing the beauty and potential held within them unless they chose to allow it to do so.

If this book helps even one individual recognize the equality in greatness with who they are in relationship to everything else imaginable in this Cosmos, then its purpose has been served.

If I can do it, so can they.

The church

The church in Ojai, California
photo by Megan Cerminaro

Young Kevin

Image of Kevin before moving to
Oregon
school photo

Evergreen Drive

The house on Evergreen Drive in Oregon.
family photo

Fallen Peppercorns: A Story of Reslilience

PART 1
Mallory Way, Ventura County, California

1.

IT WAS THURSDAY afternoon, mid-December, 1973. "Do you think we can make a few more bike ramps?" I asked my brother. I kicked the fallen leaves laying on the street as we walked the mile home from school. The wind blew calmly from the east and leaves danced on the pavement, whispering a poetic rustle as they pirouetted and twirled about. The air was cool, but not cold. The sky was bright and cast an afternoon glow of orange on an open field as we headed down the rural road.

Steve did not reply to my question. I wanted to inquire again but resisted when I noticed that his gaze was focused on something off in the distance, something which I could not see. The faint smell of dinner emanated from one of the houses that we passed by. The subtle sound of a television played from within. A wooden fence, washed with the orange-hued light from the afternoon sun, obscured the house's windows and kept us from looking in. The same orange sunlight shone on my brother's face, a face darkened with emotion.

Steve was active in school sports and extremely competitive. His competitiveness bordered on aggression, an aggression that some interpreted as anger. He intimidated many kids, including me, and his ambitious nature affected our relationship. Our father, for unexplained reasons, believed that it was best to keep his kids' scholastic activities separate, and had therefore enrolled our three younger brothers – Tim, Pat, and Terry in different elementary schools around the valley. But for some reason, that hadn't applied to Steve and me. We both went to Nordhoff High School in Ojai.

"Yeah, but let's make them bigger this time," he replied after a delay. "And tell your friend Tom the next time he tries to play my guitar I'm gonna pound him," Steve snapped at me.

"Okay," I mumbled with a hint of sarcasm.

Tom was one of my school buddies. One way that Steve displayed his dominance was to make sure that his brother's friends knew how to behave in our home. He frequently threatened to beat up anyone who didn't show him the proper respect that he felt he deserved.

Steve walked at my side, but at a distance. His hair had grown over his ears and was being blown back by the wind, exposing sideburns rarely found on a person of his age. He glanced my way and smirked, suppressing a chuckle as if to imply he wasn't angry with me.

As we walked by the stoic Presbyterian church with its newly whitewashed walls, the fragrance from the eucalyptus trees that lined its borders floated towards us on the cool eastern breeze and softened Steve's off-key singing of Don McLean's *American Pie*.

"Do you think we could get into the church by that back door over there?" he questioned.

"Let's try," I said with a mixture of excitement and trepidation.

As we scampered across the well-groomed lawn, my heart beat loudly in my chest. Any time that I followed Steve into an illegal venture of any type, my gut ached. It was as if it was trying to speak to me. That hesitancy birthed a degree of fear in me, but I pushed it aside and continued on. "You go. Try the door but be quiet," whispered Steve.

I reached for the well-worn latch. Its metal was cold to the touch. It would not move. I tried repeatedly. The fragrance of the eucalyptus leaves seemed to intensify in accordance with my heart rate. I turned to Steve who was looking over his shoulder, distracted by an older couple walking on the sidewalk, deep in conversation. The fairly consistent car traffic on the street in front of the church meant that timing was of the essence if we were not to be caught. Steve turned toward me and I shook my head, indicating that the door would not open.

"We'll come back later," he whisper-shouted in my direction.

Suddenly, I heard what sounded like an irregular clapping noise. It was very soft, not mechanical, but similar to the sound created by the subtle striking of hands or of flesh hitting a hard surface. It seemed to be coming from the trees near the rear of the church. I grew apprehensive and quickly moved away from the door, its size and the darkly stained wood loomed over me, exaggerated by my heightened emotions. I ran back from the sanctuary to the sidewalk where my brother waited and told Steve about the noise I'd heard.

"Really. Did you see anyone? Let's come back later," he said with a grin. The wind had turned chilly and the shadows had grown long. There was an ominous feeling in the air.

"I'll run to the corner and you throw me a bomb!" I shouted, in effort to lighten the mood. I took off at a sprint and prepared to catch his imaginary pass.

"Go deep!" Steve shouted back. As Steve made a throwing motion, I was distracted from my catch. I'd glanced up the street where our house resided and noticed a small car parked hastily along the curb, opposing traffic and blocking our driveway.

Steve shouted as he ran past me, heading in the direction of the lot. He must not have seen the car. He sprinted past me on my left and as the distance between us increased, so did the quiet beauty of the trees and the lightly dusted ridge of the snow-capped Topa Topa mountains in the distance. These majestic giants cradled the small valley town of Ojai, like a mother holding her baby. Steve's small silhouette put into perspective the grandeur of the mountains, and at that moment, I felt gratitude for the idyllic setting that I called home.

As we approached the visiting car, I noticed a small metal cross hanging from its rearview mirror. The front seat was covered with pamphlets and papers, and the upholstery was well-worn and faded, similar to the car's factory paint. I could tell that the vehicle had not been parked long as the distinctive sound of the cooling engine could be heard from under the hood. To me, it seemed like the little sedan proudly boasted its many years of servitude.

"Come on!" Steve yelled, stifling his frustration with me.

As we approached the house, things seemed quieter than usual. A breeze danced through the branches of the giant pepper tree that enveloped the front yard of our house. The silence was broken only by the creaking branches and the noise of scattering red peppercorns which, once fallen, blanketed the worn and displaced brick walk leading up to the front door. The tree was old and had deep taproots. It had withstood the test of time and had experienced many seasons there along the sidewalk on Mallory Way. I had respect for that old tree and had spent many a day beneath its branches. It had become a friend of mine and I'd always wondered what it would say if it could talk? I paused briefly and gazed up at its magnificence before continuing to the front door.

Like so many other times, with rambunctious children present, the door had been left wide open. As I crossed the threshold, I noticed an unfamiliar man, plainly clothed and standing in the living room near the entrance to the kitchen. He appeared relaxed, small in stature, and leaned a bit awkwardly to one side. He had his arms placed behind his back, his hands interlocked. His gaze was unyielding and followed my every movement as I entered the house. The afternoon sunlight that streamed through the open door painted the bottom of his faded, tattered jeans, and I gathered that he must be a man of meager means. At his feet sat five relatively large cardboard boxes that glowed in the pink light of the afternoon sun.

"Hello, young man. I am Minister Ferrerez of the Presbyterian church," he said softly as he extended his trembling arm to ask for a handshake. The tremor suggested a burden of some sort, perhaps a serious health problem. I wondered how he'd gotten to our house before we had. Certainly, he was here because of our entry attempt into his church, but he said nothing about it. He paused and his glance went elsewhere. I followed his gaze to the front door, where I locked eyes with Steve. "Kevin, what are you doing?"

"You must be Steven, the oldest?" the minister asked.

"Yeah," he blurted back. "What do you want?"

At that moment, I realized that our three younger brothers were also present. Two stood with their backs against the old gas heater situated to the right of the front door. The gas flame heated two vertical steel tubes and when doing so, made the tubes snap sharply, like the sound of gravel being thrown on a tin roof. The sound echoed a belligerent chorus during the momentary lapse of silence. My younger brothers stood still, except for the occasional shift in body weight due to the aggressive heater's output. The heater also produced a sharp metallic odor, not displeasing, but noticeable. This odor permeated the room and mingled with the scent of a sink-full of unwashed dishes. Though open, the airflow from the front door failed to dispel the stench of the combined odors.

My brother Terry, a diligent reader, stood behind me to my left, grasping a superhero comic book. His posture suggested that the presence of the minister was a matter of urgency. I looked over my shoulder to Steve, wide-eyed with apprehension, sure that we'd been caught.

"I'm here for your mother," the minister said. "She has been admitted to the hospital for a nervous break-down and arrangements for you kids have been made. Your father and his wife were notified that the five of you will be arriving in Portland, Oregon by bus tomorrow evening. They should be there to pick you up. Some assistants from the church and I took the liberty to pack what we considered to be essential for you, we did our best to assume which articles belong to each of you. You each have one box. This is all we could do with the short time frame that we have to work with."

As the man spoke, he leaned over, pointing to the boxes. His hand trembled as if struggling against an in-surmountable weight. He wore a large grey cross which hung from his neck, like a pendulum held by an anxious dowser's hand. His face looked as if he'd fallen victim to either too much sun or alcohol, or perhaps both. Capil-laries covered his skin in a fine spider-webbed pattern, but did not hide its deep creases and fine lines.

"Can we see our mom?" asked Pat, teary-eyed.

"She does not want to see you boys, not at this time," the minister replied with a sigh. "We need to leave immediately as your bus is scheduled to leave Ventura in one hour."

"What about our pets?" Pat pleaded. "My friend David is supposed to come by. Can we at least say goodbye to our mommy?" His confusion tumbled out all at once.

"No, we need to leave now," the minister replied quite sternly.

As we walked towards his dilapidated car, I stumbled on one of the loose bricks in the walkway and struggled to regain composure. In pausing, I noticed that the great pepper tree was quiet now. The breeze no longer caressed its grandiose branches. I yearned for it to speak to me, to tell us what to do. Our cat, Suzi Wang, named after a character in a story we liked, watched intently from a tree limb above. As silent and confused as we were, she observed the only humans she'd ever known to fill her food dish, go.

With boxes in each of our laps, the small sedan strained to accommodate all six passengers. The exhaust system needed attending to and fumes permeated the interior of the car. The fumes mixed with the musty smell of the torn cloth seats challenged one's olfactory senses. The car required full attention from its driver, the wheels felt as if they were out of balance. The engine strained with its cargo as if to groan a message, one perhaps the minister already knew deep down. I glanced at the strewn pamphlets scattered on the rusted, bare metal floor, its carpet long since worn away. One of these pamphlets stood out to me. On it, emblazoned in bold red print, was 'TREAT THOSE AS YOU WISH TO BE TREATED.' The corners were bent and smudges on the paper suggested that it had been offered many times by a well-meaning trembling hand, only to be rejected.

The atmosphere in the car was solemn, punctuated with the gentle sobs of confused children who'd just been torn from the only home they'd ever known. We tried to muster the maturity of adults, but we had not yet experienced enough years to develop it. Unsure of what to expect once we arrived at our destination, we were scared and unsettled.

Little did we know, we would not be greeted by open arms or the faintest amount of love. Our newfound home would challenge every ounce of our survivability. It would forever leave its imprint on our budding spirits and redefine our perceptions of family and love. Each of us would face trauma and be forever transformed. Clackamas County Oregon and its community were about to witness events unfathomable to most. Especially those who believed in a just and loving creator.

2.

IT WAS MONDAY morning in the early spring of 1969. I awoke to Steve's pestering.

"You gonna get up? We should get going or mom will get pissed." He was in a hurry to get to school, not for academic purposes, but to see a young gal that he was courting. He sat on his small, unmade bed. His back was to me and his faded corduroy pants were wrinkled and hastily thrown on. The skin on his shirtless back indicated puberty, that awkward time when so many of us handed over our hard-earned money to topical acne medication companies in hopes of relief. He stared out of the window with interest. The bedroom window was positioned such that it looked inside the enclosed screen porch attached to the rear of our house. Cobwebs hung lazily in dusty corners. The morning light was soft, blanketed by an early morning fog which was common in the Ojai Valley in Spring.

"Are you hanging out with Jackie today?" I asked. My mouth was dry as I spoke like I had been exposed for a prolonged time in an arid, parched environment.

"Yeah. I don't think her old man likes me too much though," he replied with a chuckle. Suddenly, I heard a thumping sound coming from outside. It was muffled, but consistent and varied in tempo from rapid to slow, and back again. I was unsure of the exact direction that it was coming from, but felt relatively confident that it was coming from the covered porch.

I slowly gathered myself and emerged from my single bed, my ankle sore from a footrace at school that I'd participated in the previous Friday. I glanced out the window and noticed my two youngest brothers, already dressed, on the far corner of the porch, adjacent to the screen door. My youngest brother, Tim, was sitting cross-legged, facing toward me. His eyes were anxious, his face dismayed. Pat stood closely, almost overtop of him. It appeared as though Pat was performing a homemade ceremony of sorts, and that Tim was being subjected to his older brother's wishes. In Pat's hand, was a small, flat paint stick that he tapped repeatedly on Tim's shoulder.

"What are those guys doing?" Steve asked as he walked from our room and into the small hallway. I watched with a degree of fascination as Pat continued rapping the paintstick on Tim's shoulder. At once, our mother called out to my youngest brothers. Only then did Pat cease his tapping. I reached for the window and pried open its creaky, gummed-up frame.

"What's up?" I asked.

"This will make mom feel better," Pat replied.

It seemed to all of us that mom had been in low spirits for the last few weeks. What I didn't know then, but I do now, is that she displayed all of the modern-day signs of depression. Where I had once shared many common interests with her, both artistic and creative, she no longer desired to engage. She'd gone from the quintessential mother, one who'd send her children to school with brown paper bag lunches with our names written in ink across the paper, to listless and apathetic. It used to be that on days when I stayed home from school, suffering from bouts of illness, I would lie on the floor, mother would rub my chest with menthol ointment, and we'd become immersed in one of the many art books she'd acquired. She'd often encourage my creative side by handing me a watercolor set or a new pencil and a pad of paper. But lately, she was different, sullen.

Our mother had been born into a strict, legalistic Lutheran family. Her father had been a plumber, her mother, a stay-at-home mom. Her younger sister maintained a strong connection to the Lutheran Church and therefore, a strong connection to their father. For reasons unknown to my brothers and me, our grandfather had disowned our mother, and us. We had been 'marked by satan.' I always wondered whether that was the beginning of my mother's deep and debilitating sense of insecurity. She never had the same relationship with her father that her sister did, and I believe that negatively impacted her self esteem. Over the years, mother searched for acceptance from her father, but found none.

Our father's given name was Richard, though he preferred to be called 'Dick.' He was an intellectual and a narcissist. These traits, combined with his repressed anger and insecurity, formed the foundation of our father's character. His behavior was also affected by his continual, daily indulgence of hard liquor. Martinis were his preferred after-work cocktail, and *Brew 102* beer satisfied him on the weekends. One might also call our father a social climber. He had no true friends in life, he only allowed acquaintances, and that rule extended even to members of his own family.

When he was one year of age, my father's mother succumbed to the horrors of brain cancer. His father, now a widower, worked as a bartender in the San Joaquin Valley. The two of them moved continuously throughout the valley to wherever our grandfather could find employment. Grandfather desired to have his son cared for by a mother figure and therefore sent our father to his sister and her husband in Portland, Oregon. Perhaps, to him, this felt like rejection, and may have contributed to his character flaws later in life. After completing high school, our father moved back to California to rejoin his father while attending junior college. My grandfather accepted him back into his home with the excitement that only a caring father could, pleased to be reunited with his son. My father lived with his father until he entered the air force.

My grandfather, on the other hand, was nothing like my dad. He was a diligent, artistic bachelor and cared deeply for his son and his grandchildren. Each summer, my excitement peaked as days elapsed, nearing the time when I got to go and visit him. During those lengthy stays, full of fun and storytelling, Grandpa would often remark on the utmost respect and pride he had for his son. I could tell, however, that he seemed hurt by my Dad's lack of desire to visit or talk to him. I was fortunate to get to spend many evenings with him, awash in stories from Homer and the *Iliad* to Mark Twain. Entwined in folklore and literature were bits of family history that I thirsted so much for. Grandpa was also a skilled painter and frequently slipped out back to his small art studio tucked betwixt the poinsettias behind his house in San Clemente. Here, he encouraged me to watch his every brushstroke, and I was fascinated as he liberated painting after painting of Mexico from his easel.

As I walked down the narrow hallway on the once-white carpet, now a grey shadow of its former self, my unlaundered shirt hung from my small shoulders like it was hanging from a clothesline. I heard a soft voice coming from my parents' room. It sounded as if my mother was upset, her voice trembling and weepy. Then the unmistakably loud baritone voice of my father penetrated through the door.

"Damnit Kathy! I am just not going to do it!" The door opened forcefully and the man we knew as our father, barreled through wearing a cheap-looking suit, expressive of his repetitive financial frustrations. This was the same suit that Dad wore to work as the school principal of Lincoln Elementary School.

I'd later find out that this was the beginning of the end for my parents. Our mother had sought-after a man who would take care of her, and allow her to be like her mother, a traditional American housewife. But she'd found our father instead. The both of them desired attention, support and acceptance from the community. But our father overshadowed and overlooked our mother. As time went on, her unhappiness in the marriage grew.

3.

IT WAS MONDAY morning in 1973, at the Mira Monte Elementary School in Ojai, California.

"Are you going to compete in the Presidential Fitness Program?" asked my neighboring classmate. We sat together and shared a desk. I glanced at the clock, as I often did over the course of the day, and thought to myself, 'only four more hours to go.'

The north wall of the classroom was constructed primarily of windows, which revealed to the class the state of the weather throughout the day. The smell of chalk dust hovered in the room and the cold linoleum floors reflected the light from an overcast sky.

"What are the three branches of the government?" asked our teacher Mr. Hoe, who stood at one side of the dusty chalkboard. He was a soft-spoken young man of slight build, who emanated kindness and was diligently passive in his behavior.

I glanced over at my neighbor's desk drawer and noticed something gleaming. It was a ball bearing that we'd use for a game of marbles. These steely orbs were prized by us, more for their sheer weight, which we preferred over their glass marble counterparts.

"Do you want to trade for your steely?" I whispered as Mr. Hoe wrote the answers to his previous test question on the board.

"What do you –" My classmate's reply was cut short by the opening of the classroom door located in the rear of the room. As I focused my gaze on the person standing in the doorway, I realized that it was the school principal, Mr. Erickson. His face was marked like a sandstone canyon and it rarely displayed a smile. His blue suit had a long necktie that seemed to fortify his presence. His frail physique, which slumped forward as if he had a weight tied around his neck, was not of a man that naturally commanded respect. He paced briskly down the edge of the room, maintaining a safe distance away from the students' desks. He headed straight for Mr. Hoe. The two talked in a low whisper without much gesturing, their backs were turned to the class. The brief meeting ended and Mr. Hoe spoke.

"Kevin, would you follow Mr. Erickson out, please?"

I got up from my desk and the classroom fell silent. I felt a lump in my throat. Suddenly nauseous, I thought that I was about to be disciplined for something, but I was not certain of what. I tailed Mr. Erickson, struggling to keep up with his long strides. He remained silent, as if I was not there. The cement walk we followed was covered by a metal roof, similar to all of the walks leading to and from the school classrooms. A smell wafted from the cafeteria kitchen and suggested fried chicken and banana pudding for lunch.

We entered the principal's office and his secretary gave a quick, obligatory smile and quickly returned her attention back to the mimeograph machine. The unmistakable odor of its ink stands out in my memory, the scent of the precursor to the modern-day copy machine. Mr. Erickson settled behind his desk and gestured for me to sit opposite him. My mind was racing in time with my pulse. I was nervous, fidgety and racked my brain for what I'd done to land me here in this seat in the Principal's office.

"Your father has asked me to relay a message to you. Your mother has demanded a divorce from him. I feel awkward delivering this news to you at school but I'm following your father's request," he quietly spoke.

My eyes wandered to the framed degrees which hung on the wall behind his shoulder and then back to his face which appeared as if it were etched, like a Rembrandt portrait. The light cast from the incandescent desk lamp sitting on his desk made his complexion appear jaundiced. The office phone rang, and the odor of the mimeograph ink intensified as I allowed his words to sink in, just as the overcast sky sunk into the valley that day.

"I'll have someone take you home," he stated as he stared intently at the paperwork lying on his desk. He avoided direct eye contact, and I understood his uneasiness with the situation.

The school employee who was given the task to drive me home spoke not a word, and the car ride seemed to drag on and on. Eucalyptus trees that lined the sides of the road seemed to run by, as if they were in a hurry to be anywhere other than where they stood. I could relate. The odor of the mimeograph ink lingered, as if fresh copies of divorce papers sat right next to me on the seat. The driver's hair was meticulously put up in a bun, stacked neatly on the back of her head. Her nails, which grasped the wheel firmly, appeared freshly manicured, perhaps waiting to be touched by the hand of a man – who knows.

The car finally stopped at the curb in front of our house, the house afflicted by unspoken turmoil. When stepping out of the vehicle, I noticed that the curb's surface was layered with peppercorns dropped by the Grand Master above. As I walked under the tree, I longed for it to break its long silence, to tell me of stories it had witnessed over the years, to offer comfort in this time of confusion. I realized that the great pepper tree was observing yet another chapter in time, the story of the dismemberment of a family who lived underneath its regal branches.

"If you could talk to me, what news would you bring?" I mentally asked the tree.

Within the month, my father would no longer resided at the pale yellow house on Mallory Way.

Once the divorce was completed, my mother was relegated to caring for five young boys, a task which proved to be too much for her both financially and mentally. As her stress swelled, so did her emotional instability. She felt shameful for taking welfare and food stamps and grew fearful of others' opinions of her.

Neighbors were frequently asked to intervene in family matters. My brothers and I were sent off to perform menial jobs, such as gardening and babysitting in efforts to help with the bills. The Department of Social Services sent people out to check on us. My father refused to obey the California Court's order to pay child support, and therefore abandoned his duty to my mother and to us. This drove her further toward madness.

I later discovered that these were the reasons that on that cold December day in 1973, in the house on Mallory Way, mom signed the final resignation note as sole caregiver to my brothers and me. That was the start to our whole ordeal. The words that passed from the minister's discolored lips, "She does not want to see you boys at this time," would reverberate in my mind for years to come, like an unbroken chain, the ends of which were held by nothing.

4.

IT WAS THURSDAY evening, 1973. We were in the back of the Minister's old battered car, en route to the bus station. A heavy silence blanketed the inside of the car, pierced only by the occasional whine of the straining engine. It sounded as if the car pleaded to retire from its mechanical life, each time the minister demanded more power by mashing his foot down on the pedal. My brothers were quiet, as if contemplating their fate. Crying was no longer a solution. It was as if we had been handed down a sentence by an unknown judge in an imaginary courtroom. The minister was solemnly quiet. The only lapse in his emotional apathy was when he'd quickly glanced back at us in the broken rearview mirror. His uneasiness with the situation was obvious, punctuated by the beads of sweat on his forehead. Undoubtedly, minutes felt like hours, or perhaps days, as he firmly grasped the steering wheel and stared straight ahead.

The sun had just begun to set over the Topa Topa Mountains as we finally arrived at the small bus terminal. There was a faded Greyhound bus sign which hung above the white stucco building. The bus was to take the five of us to our new home, or so we were told. Come to find out, that term had been grossly misused. The place we were going to was more like a prison.

When I opened the door of the car, a sharp metallic noise resonated, as if in warning. The minister emerged from his door and moved quickly to the rear of the car and popped the trunk, before catching a beat. One by one, he quickly set our boxes down on the sidewalk. The tremor in his arm increased in intensity, which caused one of the boxes to slip. It awkwardly landed with a soft thud. As we stood on the sidewalk, he gave a half-hearted wave and disappeared into the musty car with tattered seats. Not a word was spoken. We had all hoped that he'd say something, anything really. I wanted him to rescind this decision, to tell us to get back into the car, or that there'd been a mistake. Alas, our hopes were dashed. The car seemed to leave the curb much more easily than it had arrived there, the burden of us lifted. It must have been a relief for the Minister to drive away.

Pat stood next to me, nervously biting his fingernails. Tim was quiet as if he'd just woke from an afternoon nap. All five of us stood there, frozen, like our emotions. We waited for someone or something to assist us, to guide us away from the cracked, weed-infested sidewalk and into our new lives, but nothing and no one came. A coastal breeze stirred discarded paper and styrofoam cups, strewn haphazardly on the surface of the pavement. As I watched the trash roll around with no apparent purpose, meaning, or direction except from that of the sea breeze, I felt a stark resemblance to that garbage. I too had been discarded. I was no more or less important than a styrofoam cup. Once required for a purpose, the cup that was no longer needed had been tossed just as carelessly as we had. Our destinations were alike, to be determined by the wind.

I gradually turned my attention back to my surroundings and noticed that my brothers had settled on one of the waiting benches outside of the small terminal building. Steve stood while the other three sat waiting, still trying to wrap their heads around the afternoon's ordeal.

My attention was then drawn to a small old man, who'd been sitting alone on one of the three other benches in front of the building. He appeared to be Mexican. His weathered face was unshaven, white sparse beard hairs sprouted unevenly across his dark face, and his long, uncombed white hair hung well over his ears. He was unusually short in stature and wore soiled white linen pants that were frayed at the seams. His pant cuffs partially hid bright red cloth tennis shoes. His blue jacket was modest and seemed to be much too big for him. But his most noticeable attribute was his green eyes that were fixed directly on mine as if he knew me. He had a certain peace about him, yet his gaze was intense. As I watched him, I could hear him softly humming to himself, reciting a song which was unfamiliar to me. Had we met before at some time? Did he recognize me?

"Are you coming over here? I have your ticket!" Steve shouted to me.

I picked up the cardboard box at my feet with the name 'Kevin' written on it in red ink and walked to where my brothers had been waiting. The old man continued to follow me with his gaze. I wondered if he would eventually speak to me. The fronds on the tall palm tree he was sitting under rustled in the breeze as if to confirm the answer to my question.

"Do you have any money on you?" Steve asked me. "I want to get some of those barbeque potato chips in that machine." I searched my pockets and found a dime and placed it in his opened hand. Pat was talking in a low whisper to Tim who was huddled close by his side. A lost look was painted on our youngest brother's face, a face which had yet to experience seven years of life. I was focused on his expression when the low roar of a diesel engine distracted me from my thoughts. A Greyhound bus came through the turn of the terminal driveway. It appeared like a lumbering dragon, weighted down by its passengers and cargo. Judging by the dirt and soot coating its big metal body, it was evident that this bus had served many people and had traveled many miles. As it moved slowly into position to unload and receive new passengers, its large tires crushed the litter that was scattered about under the bus's mighty weight. The styrofoam cup that I'd felt akin to just moments ago, was flattened.

A few minutes passed and an announcement was made through a loudspeaker to board the bus. Few passengers disembarked and my brothers and I made up five of the seven new passengers. As my brothers climbed up the bus steps, I glanced back towards the bench where the old man had been sitting. He was gone, but had left a few small items behind on the bench seat where he'd sat just moments before. I was unsure if he had forgotten them or if he no longer wanted his things. I quickly made my way over to the bench, and scanned in all four directions for him. Aware of how little time I had before my departure, I grabbed the man's things and took off. One was a small package, perhaps four inches long, wrapped in a white paper napkin secured tightly with a rubber band. The other was a small flat, glass flask. The wrapped object was particularly light in weight. I had no time to unwrap it so I shoved it into my pocket on the way back to the bus. I climbed up the steps and entered the beast of a bus, my eyes strained to find an available seat. While scanning for a spot to spend the next twenty-one hours, I noticed the intermittent coughing and crying of multiple children. I found in the very rear of the bus, a bench seat where two of my brothers already sat. The bus doors closed, finalizing our fate. As the beast eased away from the terminal, my brothers and I watched the orange street lights that lined the road, tick slowly by the window, one by one.

Approximately fifteen minutes after our departure, I remembered the man's things in my pocket and quietly removed the bottle and placed it into the box at my feet. I then reached into my pocket to investigate the object that was wrapped in the paper napkin. I held it for a while, rolling it back and forth over my palm before I unwrapped it. I took the rubber band off and slowly unfurled the torn napkin. It was a small pipe. It appeared to be quite old and was made of some type of clay with remnants of a pale yellow paint on its surface. Its edges were well worn and smooth, revealing a brown earthen material from which it was made. The bowl of the pipe was a very odd shape. It was relatively small and had a narrow neck which felt very warm to the touch. I shrugged and placed it back into my pocket, not realizing in that moment what an impact this small object would have in my future.

PART 2
Evergreen Drive, Clackamas County Oregon

5.

IT WAS LATE Friday evening on a December night. The passengers' fatigue seemed to weigh down the bus more than the cargo it held. After the wheels laboriously passed twenty-one hours over pavement, we'd finally arrived at our destination. Portland, Oregon appeared like a blanket of light laid over a darkened landscape.

"I think we're here," Pat said, announcing our arrival to anyone listening. My legs and back were stiff. I felt empty, as if I'd left my emotions far behind us, at the bus depot back in Ventura. As we pulled into the fluorescently lit bus terminal, the top of the beast nearly touched the low-hanging depot ceiling. I was surprised when it didn't scrape the bus's roof off. The air brakes hissed, declaring that this was the beast of a bus's final resting place. People began to stir and shake the sleep from their tired bodies. Folks were slow to move, most everyone had to wait for the circulation to re-enter their legs. I sat in my seat, waiting. I was hesitant to move, fearful of what lay ahead once we departed the bus terminal. Steve was the first brother to rise from his seat a few rows ahead of us. He looked like a disgruntled employee en route to clock in for a long shift of a dislikable job.

"Let's go guys," he said without so much as a glance in our direction. His words were monotone, without emotion, as if he too had left his feelings back in Ventura. It felt like we were about to surrender to the enemy. Tim watched Steve and Pat intently, mimicking his brother's movements, as if he were a newborn baby, mirroring the actions of his mother. He followed closely behind Pat down the narrow bus aisle, and then they both disappeared from sight when they stepped down the steps and off of the bus. The bus was now quiet with no occupants, except for me. I remained in my seat which had supported me for nearly one full day. I listened to the silence that filled the bus, its seats now quiet, lonesome. The stillness was broken by an announcement by the dispatcher over the Portland terminal speaker. Finally, I peeled myself from the crusty bus seat and walked down the aisle. As I slowly walked, I gazed through the scummy windows at the scant number of people wandering around the terminal. They were employees, mostly. I imagined what their lives were like. What kind of families did they have? What were their homes like? Were they from a happy home, or a broken one? Was anyone there to greet them after a long workday?

Once out of the bus, fluorescent depot lights burned my eyes. I had to squint to soften the visual blow until they adjusted. My cardboard box with my few possessions was the last item of luggage left on the cement sidewalk. Every other passenger had already claimed their belongings. Though my brothers were present, I felt totally alone in that moment. I picked up my box and walked through the glass doors and into the lobby of the bus depot. There, my brothers stood around a man who appeared to be troubled, disturbed. He too grappled with a decision that had been made by another. Here was our father.

The minister's decision to send us to Oregon had ruptured our father's home. It had alarmed his new wife and her two children. Not only would the five of us require clothing, but we'd need food and shelter as well. Overnight, our dad's long-desired dream of getting out from under the burden of debt, went up in smoke. Perhaps he thought he'd conveniently left his past with his ex-wife in California. But children are much more perceptive than adults give them credit for. Was this a psychological game of chess? Did our parents, two divorced adults who despised each other just enough, plan to use us as pawns in their sick little game of revenge? 'Pawn to Queen Bishop 4,' I thought. Then I wondered, did mother really have a nervous breakdown? Or was she trying to get back at dad by sending us to Oregon?

Not much was said from the time that we met our father, exited the depot and loaded into his maroon Volkswagen van that was parked in the "No-loading Zone" immediately outside of the terminal entrance. Our father's wife, Lynn, was sitting in the passenger's seat.

"How are you boys?" she asked quietly.

"We're tired," Terry replied, as we nervously shifted our bodies on the car's bench seat. He usually kept quiet. Terry did not often volunteer information or participate in conversation unless it was important. He was logical and strategic, even at a young age. Tim sat on the floor, holding his box of possessions on his lap. Our cardboard boxes were now our only lifeline back to the home we once knew in California.

"Jesus, you kids look a mess. You are already registered for school. Steve, you'll be going to Beavercreek High. Kevin and Terry will be at Gardner Junior High and Pat and Tim will be at Beavercreek Elementary. I want you all to get haircuts," Dad said, as if reading from a pre-written script. I was in ninth grade. In California, I had been in high school with Steve, but in Oregon, ninth grade was still junior high.

"Dick, I think they should have some clothes for school," Lynn interjected.

"God damn it! Don't we have enough to deal with right now?" he barked.

The silence was deafening as the van's wheels sang on the wet road, soaked by a recent rainstorm. You could cut through the tension in the car. We had neither been invited nor wanted by our dad or Lynn. The car's headlights sliced through the mist lingering above the road's surface as we passed by dark forests. I watched the dark silhouettes of trees go by, hidden by the absence of sunlight, and wondered what this new landscape looked like in the midst of day?

"Are you kids hungry?" Lynn asked as she turned her head towards us. There was dead silence. All five of us hesitated to say a thing for we'd just been given guilt, the gift that keeps on giving.

"Yes," Steve mumbled meekly. "Don't lean on me so hard, give me some room," He then said to me. I shifted closer to the window, trying to give him space. Suddenly, I became aware of my body odor. One can imagine what five young, anxious boys stuffed on a bus for twenty-one hours, smelled like. The odor in the van added to the discomfort of everyone.

After forty-five minutes, the Volkswagen slowed down and took a right turn. I noticed a green road sign briefly illuminated by the headlights, 'Evergreen Drive.' The car followed the small one-lane road for a few minutes and the landscape outside appeared even more dark and foreboding than before. There were a few lights emitting from windows of the sparsely scattered homes along the way. This was the only indication that people inhabited this seemingly remote area.

The vehicle slowed and the pavement turned to gravel. As we rounded another soft sweeping corner, the lights of our final destination came into view. I imagined a curtain lifting on a dark stage, lights abruptly illuminating, the stage set to present a play to the world, and we were the actors. This was it, the home where we were to reside for the next six months or longer.

To this day, I feel a degree of sympathy for that house. Its purpose was to be a home to people, to shelter and bring comfort to its inhabitants. A noble purpose, if you ask me. And if a house could feel, I imagine it would be pleased to be needed and happy to be taken care of. Better still if the people within it felt the same. I still feel for that house, for what it experienced after our arrival. And I hope to this day that it has recovered from us, from the things it had to witness and the anger and grief that it endured. If walls could talk, I hope they'd say that they have healed from their trauma, and I hope that its current occupants feel loved and cared for. A house deserves to feel that its walls and roof have served a useful purpose. A well-loved house becomes more than a four-walled structure, it becomes a home. It witnesses family and friends growing up and growing old together. Best wishes for that house, I hope all is well for it now.

6.

THE VOLKSWAGEN pulled into the dimly lit garage and stopped. After our father killed the engine, a sobering silence hung heavily inside the van. Slowly, we gathered up our things and exited the vehicle without speaking a word. I glanced toward the driver's seat, half expecting some sort of direction from our father, but he'd already gone. The garage was damp and musty. Lynn gestured for us to follow her through the garage door and into the house. It seemed as though we'd entered into a small dark cellar, and it took me a moment to gauge our location.

Attached to the garage was a dim, narrow hallway. Lynn walked a few steps and stopped in front of a door. With the likeness of a traffic guard, she motioned to Steve and me with her left arm. This was our room. Shyly, we stepped inside.

The room was lit by a solitary ceiling light covered by a dirty glass shade. There were two small, narrow single beds placed opposite one another. Both looked as though they'd been taken from a World War II hospital. Their metal head and foot rails had lost most of their original white paint, and the thin single mattresses which laid on their frames were stained and tattered. Each bed had a single Pendleton wool blanket and small pillow. Against a lonely wall was a single wooden dresser, its drawers sagged and buckled. The floor's surface was covered with a thinly worn linoleum and the edges had begun to curl. It was a pale green color with an odd pattern on its dingy surface, the shine long since vanished. The scene was reminiscent of a Van Gogh painting, the one he did of a shabby room in the Saint Paul Hospital with a lone bed. There was a solitary unframed window, void of a view, except that of the total darkness of night.

"I'm taking this bed," Steve proclaimed as he dropped his box atop it. Lynn had gone to direct my three younger brothers to their room. Afterwards, I silently watched her walk briskly down the dark hall in her long coat, and turn to climb the stairs to where she, her two children and our father resided. Once the coast was clear, I timidly tip-toed down the hallway, careful not to alert the owners of the house. The hallway's bare cement floor made it cold and unwelcoming. The hallway opened into a larger room, dimly lit by a small table lamp in the far corner. The floor was covered with green outdoor carpeting. It reminded me of the astroturf used on a miniature golf course. Once upon a time, we'd played miniature golf to celebrate birthdays, but I feared that was now a thing of the past. There was an outdated television console placed next to a sliding glass door which led out to the rear of the house. Its wooden finish was sullied by years of abuse. I walked toward the glass door which went outside and the blackness beyond the glass amplified my reflection. In the glass, I saw a thin young teen, who had lost his identity, sense of place and spirit. A stranger in a strange house, my brothers were all I had left to link me to any remnant of self-recognition.

"There is some food on the table up here for you guys," Lynn announced from the top of the stairs. My brothers and I climbed the stairs in a single file. Our steps were cushioned by plush carpet which covered the step's surfaces. The temperature rose remarkably and as we reached the top of the stairs. When we arrived, I looked around to behold an entirely different home. It was furnished with cozy chairs and well designed tables. Paintings hung from the freshly painted walls and soft music lulled from a stereo set which sat in one corner. There was a faint scent of a disinfectant, similar to an air freshener used in a public restroom. The kitchen was to the immediate left and a very large, wooden dining room table was located adjacent to the kitchen. Lynn's son peered out of his room, like a shy animal, tentative to the presence of someone unknown. He quickly retreated upon Lynn's command for him to get back to bed.

"I want to be clear that you need to ask permission before you come up here. And I want this area cleaned when you are finished," Lynn said in an authoritative tone as she motioned to the dining room table. She quickly turned away, as though she had been interrupted from a previous activity, and returned back to her room. We sat at the large wooden table where five metal plates sat holding small portions of Hamburger Helper, and a little biscuit. Choosing our seats at random, we felt like prisoners in a penal cafeteria. When we spoke, our words were inadvertently cloaked in whispers, fearing punishment if our talking were to be detected. Our portions were small and the meal lasted no more than five minutes.

As we took our plates into the kitchen, I noticed its cleanliness. There were shining appliances and various succulents in pretty planters that hung in beaded macrame from the ceiling. I cautiously crept towards the refrigerator, as if I was doing something illegal, and opened the door. It was stocked full of various perishables. Terry glanced into the fridge as I held the door open and quietly exclaimed "Wow!"

"Let's go." We're not supposed to be up here," I exclaimed, with a sarcastic tone. We'd gotten plenty of subtle, and some not so subtle, clues that we were not welcome in this house. We quickly descended the stairs back into the basement. We were miners, descending into a deep dark shaft without hardhats or headlamps. Our bodies had adjusted to the warmth of the upstairs, and we immediately felt chilled when our feet struck the icy, unyielding surface of the concrete floor below. It took a little while before we acclimatized to our new location, which was such a stark contrast from the environment above.

"I don't like this place," Tim murmured as tears ran down his face. Pat remained quiet. He had always been the one who pacified situations. He was the family peacekeeper, sensitive toward others, always wanting to please. He would give the shirt off of his back, or his last hard-earned dime to anyone, even a stranger. The five of us convened in the room that was allocated to Steve and me, as if we were about to hold a conference.

"We'll be okay Peanut," Steve said to Tim with a shaky air of confidence. I examined the stark room, my eyes observed every detail. There was an electric wall heater adjacent to the door. Its thermostat knob had since been removed, denying us a way to adjust the heat. My eyes kept scanning and landed on the only window in the room.

"Check it out. It's snowing," I said.

Flakes had already begun to accumulate on the corners of the sill. We were all fixated on that window for a moment, wordless, trying to comprehend the events of the last few days. Our hearts and minds were still back in Ojai, but our depleted, cold bodies were now in a freezing basement one thousand miles away from home.

It was Saturday morning. I opened my eyes from a restless sleep, and attempted to get my bearings in the strange room. Slowly, the reality of my situation set in. The cold room with two small beds and empty walls came into vision. My body felt sore, rigid, as if I was physically immobile. The faint sound of coughing could be heard, and I remembered my brothers in the next room. Steve's unmade bed was empty. He was already in the shower. It was much colder than what I was accustomed to in southern California. I glanced out the window and for the first time laid eyes on the surrounding landscape. There was about a foot of freshly fallen snow that covered the evergreen trees surrounding the property. A small meadow behind the house led into the forest, it was remarkably beautiful. I dressed hastily and took off to explore our new surroundings. As I passed the closed door of the bathroom, I heard the shower running. In the large room which I'd briefly scanned last night, I noticed the green covering on the floor was much more worn and faded than I'd previously observed. The morning sunlight peeked through the sliding glass door. I approached it to look outside and felt the glorious heat from the sun soak my entire body. I drank in the warmth like a thirsty child. My eyes were captivated by the view outside, and my body was entranced by the heat from the sunlight trickling in.

"Your turn if you want to take a shower," Steve said as he stood behind me, drying his hair with a towel.

"What do you think?" I replied, referring to our new situation.

"I don't know. I know that I'm starving." He said as he walked down the hallway.

The bathroom was small and still warm from the moisture of Steve's shower. As the hot water from the showerhead struck my skin, I was transported to a place of peace and serenity. Time slipped away as the pain and coldness left my body. The tranquility was broken by a loud knocking on the door.

"Kevin, let's go! Lynn will cut your hair and then we will go and get you boys some decent clothes," my father said forcefully. I promptly dried myself and got dressed. As I left the bathroom I noticed Tim sitting in a chair in the large room. He was facing the sliding glass door, a towel draped over his shoulders, Lynn was at work with a pair of scissors. As I watched my youngest brother sit quietly, observing the scenery beyond the confines of the glass, I realized just how young his face looked. This poor seven year old boy was being forced to step into adult-sized shoes, expected to abruptly change his frame of mind, and grow up much too quickly. He was still too young to conceive what a family unit was supposed to represent. And he was trying to be as brave as possible in the face of his new living situation. Lynn told him to sit still. Her patience was running thin. The unexpected additions to her family undoubtedly wore on her nerves.

Lynn's dream of a happy home with a career man in education, and father figure to her two young children from a previous marriage, was shattered overnight. Her disappointment in losing this dream manifested in anger and frustration. She resented the five of us, for suddenly dropping into her life and dashing her hopes for happiness.

"Lynn, where are my pants goddammit? We have to get going!" Our father shouted from upstairs. He'd accepted the superintendent job at the Colton School District, in a rural community located about twenty miles away. He was crass and irritable. And I knew it was because he thought he was free of the children he never wanted in the first place.

The agenda for the day was for us to get haircuts and new clothing. "I don't want any of my school associates to see my kids looking like they do right now. You guys are an embarrassment. Can't you at least wash the clothes that you have on? Jesus!" He lectured as we rode into town.

After our brief, but direct shopping trip to town, we returned home each with a new shirt and pair of pants. "Take care of those. I won't continue to spend money on new clothing if you abuse them," our father said as he stepped out of the vehicle.

In an attempt to soothe my youngest brother, Pat leaned over to Tim and spoke quietly, "It'll be okay," as he took the new clothes from Tim's lap.

We dropped our clothes in our rooms and rushed out to explore the freshly fallen snow. Snow was new to us, as the California climate we were used to had never provided us with the white fluffy substance. I took the afternoon to explore the property surrounding the house. There was a mild slope from the back porch that broadened into a meadow surrounded by large evergreen trees that acted as a fence line bordering the property. We walked to the west, perhaps a few hundred feet and discovered a small creek. The snow fell periodically from the tree's branches as we made our way through the forest, dampening our hair and wetting our coats. The air was damp but fragrant. We chucked snowballs at one another and constructed a snowman under one of the large pine trees. We then reluctantly headed back to the house, dragging our cold, wet feet as we went. As we plodded in soaking wet tennis shoes, I pondered our future.

"What do you think school will be like here?" I asked everyone.

"I don't know. I hope they have good looking girls," Steve said with a laugh.

Steve and I went back to our room and reminisced about our friends back in Ojai. I had been deeply disappointed that my planned Christmas trip to Disneyland with my best friend, Jules, had been cancelled due to my unexpected departure. There were no signs in our basement dwelling of the holiday's fast approach. There was not one single decoration. The only semblance of the holiday season was upstairs; however we needed an invitation to glimpse the Christmas tree that was adorned with flashing, colored lights.

"Dinner!" shouted Lynn's daughter, Michelle, from the top of the stairs. At eleven years of age, she was an introverted and quiet girl. We had very little interaction with her or her brother. I was unsure if that was because they'd been given orders by their mother to stay away from us, or if they were simply reluctant to interact with us on their own accord. Per usual, the table was set with five metal plates, each with a meager portion of Hamburger Helper and a lone biscuit. It was evident that our father and his new family had no desire to share their dinner time with us. The family on the second floor ate proper meals. Unwashed dishes in the sink suggested spaghetti and steak had been served that evening. More buffeting to me was my father's deliberate social and physical distance from us. It seemed that *his* family lived upstairs.

My hunger was not satisfied by the small portion we were given for dinner so I decided to investigate the contents of the refrigerator. "Do you guys want me to look for more food?" I whispered quietly. Steve's immediate upheaval from his chair was his answer. I followed close behind him as we entered the kitchen. He slowly opened the refrigerator door and we were instantly disappointed by the nearly empty interior. There were the remnants of one head of iceberg lettuce, half of a loaf of bread, mustard and a small amount of a prepared cheese product. I scoured through the cabinets and found a box of powdered milk and one opened bag of flour. Steve and I looked at each other hopelessly. Words were not required for what we already knew. My younger brothers came in carrying their plates and we proceeded to wash up. We then returned to our rooms, still hungry.

7.

IT WAS MONDAY morning, the first day of new schools for each of us. Steve, Terry and I were to meet the bus at the corner of the street which was about a quarter of a mile from the house. We were allowed to go upstairs to the kitchen to have breakfast, but it was a waste of time. Non-fat powdered milk provided little substance to five growing boys and could hardly be considered breakfast. It was dark and very quiet when we left the house in the mornings. We talked about Ojai and the friends that we'd left behind as we walked on the snow-lined road, shrouded in darkness. The road cut through a forest and an icy wind rustled the tree branches, chilling us to the bone. I felt a deep sadness that was intensified by the darkness and wind as we walked.

Our bus stop was the first stop on the driver's route, so we were greeted by an empty bus. Terry and Steve were engrossed in conversation when we stepped onto the bus. They continued their dialog as they found a seat. I selected to sit behind them. The bus meandered along rural roads and made its routine stops, the seats slowly filled with children and daylight began to gently peak above the tree-lined fields. After fifteen minutes elapsed, the bus stopped at a rural crossroad, and a frail-looking boy struggled up the steps and chose a seat alone up front, directly behind the bus driver. I could see that he was fitted with a permanent leg brace. I noticed how reluctant he was to make eye contact with any of the other kids as others loaded up and walked past him. Everyone passed him by, all seemed to be reluctant to sit next to him.

"Hey. I'm Howard. Who are you?" asked a short-haired boy as he sat down next to me. He was energetic, almost hyperactive. His legs moved constantly and his hands tapped a beat on the back of the seat as he spoke.

"I'm Kevin," I replied.

"Where are you from?" he asked.

"Ojai," I said. Howard looked surprised.

"Ohio?" he asked.

"No, Ojai. It's in California. Who is that kid up in the front?" I asked as I pointed to the boy with the leg brace.

"Oh him? That's Sherman. He's really weird. A real geek. He was born deformed," he said as he turned away from me and into another conversation with the kids sitting across the aisle.

I stared forward at Sherman. He gazed out of the window as if in a trance. He was the only one sitting alone on the entire bus. All of the other seats were filled, some with as many as three children. As I watched him, I wondered about his story, and imagined that he had a mother who cared deeply for him. She clothed, sheltered and fed him, perhaps giving him extra attention due to his handicap. She must have felt his emotional pain, pain that he experienced on a daily basis, and felt helpless that she was not able to change his circumstances. I wondered if she wept at times, feeling sadness for her son? The care and compassion a parent must feel for their child, captivated me. Perhaps because I did not receive that care. I wondered what it must feel like? Sherman stirred emotions in me that I wasn't aware I had. I turned away from Howard and faced the window so he couldn't see my tears.

When we approached the school, I could see the other buses lined up on the front drive, children piling off one by one. I got up when it was my turn and walked slowly down the aisle behind Terry. I asked him to meet me in front of the building as soon as school let out. Sherman remained in his seat, conscious of his disability and how it would hamper the flow of children unloading the bus. As I passed him, I said hello. A look of surprise washed over his face as he turned towards me. His lips moved in reply but they made no sound.

Upon entering the unfamiliar school, I became disoriented. I held my class schedule in my hand, which father had given to me before the weekend, looking at it for clues to the location of my first class. My two brothers had already disappeared from sight. The halls were crowded with kids who were already familiar with their bearings, some stared at me as they passed. I was the new kid, and felt more out of place with every minute that slowly drew by.

At noon, the lunch bell rang. Classes were dismissed and I followed the flow of kids to the cafeteria, tables already teamed with kids eating from lunch trays and paper sacks. The noise level in the cafeteria surged as if the whole school had just been let out on recess. I sat at the far end of a table and grew increasingly awkward. I felt out of place, just as Sherman must have felt.

"Hi, I'm Cindy. Where are you from?" asked the girl who sat across from me.

"California," I replied.

"My grandparents are from there. Here!" she said as she passed a note to me. She then ran off, giggling, back to her friends. A phone number with her name was written on the note.

The person next to me had since left, leaving their half-empty food tray behind. He had touched only the chicken and had left the salad, fruit and buttered bread. I felt lucky. It was as if he'd known of my situation and left the food as a kind gesture. I slid the trey in front of me and instantly felt better about my surroundings. The food tasted better than it looked. I didn't recall that lettuce tasted so sweet. At first I was confused, but before I could give it much thought, I'd already cleaned the tray. Evidently there was no such seasoning that could make food taste more delicious than a strong appetite. In that moment, I began to have a new appreciation for food, something which would stay with me for the rest of my life.

It was four o'clock and I met Terry on the front walk where the school buses lined the curb. "How was your day?" I asked.

"It was okay," he replied. He was always even-keeled and accepted situations as they were. I was not aware of my admiration of this quality in those days, but as I grew older, I began to appreciate him more. Terry was mature beyond his thirteen years.

After school adjourned, evening darkness quickly shrouded the bus as it retraced the rural roads back to Evergreen Drive. It was typical of northwest winters to be dark and gloomy. Bus seats emptied little by little at each stop until only my brothers and I were left. The ride became hauntingly quiet, broken only by the occasional moaning of the bus when we hit uneven patches of pavement. Though two of my brothers were present, I felt very alone, as though the bus might never stop and we'd continue on for eternity with no destination in sight. When it finally did stop, we languidly descended and began our walk down the damp, dark road to the less than welcoming residence that awaited us.

While walking, I began questioning who I was. I felt as if I was an uninvited guest at a party, thrown begrudgingly by a group of folks that felt obligated to host but, sincerely, did not want company. What was it about me that made my parents not want me? Perhaps they were ashamed of me? I was trying to reconcile how or what I could do for them to accept me enough to care for me. I thought of Sherman and wept uncontrollably. The trees were quiet as we walked, my brothers were far ahead of me by this time. I stepped onto the gravel drive to the house and noticed light coming from the upstairs windows. It was a stark comparison to the absence of light from the floor where we resided beneath. I entered the front door and climbed up the stairs to find my two brothers already sitting at the table with their plates. The portions seemed even smaller than the day before, perhaps the size of my hunger shrank the helpings of hamburger.

"How'd you guys like school?" I asked.

"Shhh! Dad just came in and yelled at us to be quiet. He also told us to do a better job cleaning the kitchen," Steve quickly remarked. We proceeded to eat our scant dinner in silence. The portions were so small, it was over in minutes.

That night seemed colder than usual. As I lay in bed, I couldn't get warm. I turned continually, trying to create as much possible heat as I could to trap under from my single Pendleton wool blanket. "Do you remember the caves we hiked to?" I asked Steve.

"Yeah. Come on though, it's better that we don't think about stuff like that. That's far away from where we are now," he said. As he spoke, I looked out the window that faced south and thought about the home I once had, laying quiet a thousand miles away. Finally, I drifted off to sleep.

8.

IT WAS SATURDAY morning in mid-January, 1974. Little did we know, this was to be one of the coldest and longest winters in Clackamas County history. I chose to remain in my bed, trying to trap as much warmth as possible inside my woolen blanket. The sole window in our bedroom was cast in frost, preventing any clear view to the outside. Steve was still asleep. Suddenly, I heard a commotion in the hall, it sounded like people were struggling with something. I peeked out of the bedroom door and noticed two men awkwardly maneuvering a dolly with what looked like a refrigerator into the laundry room located next to our bathroom.

"What's going on?" Steve asked, disrupted from his slumber.

"I don't know. It looks like two guys are moving a refrigerator into the laundry room," I said softly. As I dressed, I noticed that the pants bought for me on Christmas no longer fit. In order to stay on my waist, I now needed a belt. I removed the one packed for me from my cardboard box and threaded it through my pant loops. Now dressed, I tip-toed down the hallway to watch the two men install the appliance.

"How are you, young fella? How do you like your new freezer?" asked one of the workers. They whisked away before I could answer, off to another job. My two younger brothers were in the large room watching television, their eyes fixed on a morning cartoon program. I joined them, yawning away the exhaustion that I felt.

"We are going into town for a while. I don't want to find anything out of place when we get back. We'll be back in a few hours," our father's voice said as he, Lynn and her two kids passed down the hallways and into the garage. We waited patiently until the noise of the Volkswagen faded over the hill, before hastily heading upstairs like scavengers in search of food scraps. This was one of the very few times the five of us would be left at home alone. I ascended the stairs two at a time, with my brothers following closely behind, to look for any food we could find. To our dismay, aside from the box of powdered milk and bag of flour, the choices were scant. Lynn had been very thorough with food storage so that it remained inaccessible to us. Pat found a few stray eggs on the countertop so I quickly tried to improvise something which might be halfway palatable. I threw what ingredients I could find together in a bowl and produced something similar to pancake batter. Terry located a frying pan and we proceeded to cook up our own version of hotcakes. Steve came up to join us and we sat together and enjoyed the fairly tasteless, but warm and filling hotcakes, without syrup of course. In that moment, I realized just how fortunate I was to have my brothers by my side during this time. We were a unit, supporting each other through what would be one of the most, if not *the* most, emotionally challenging time of our lives.

Steve stood abruptly, pulled by curiosity, and announced that he was going to explore the forbidden upstairs. I tentatively followed along. As we ascended the stairs to the second floor of the house, our bodies tingled with the warmth so plentiful on this floor. He opened the first door on the right and we determined that this must be Michelle's room. It was well furnished with a bed covered in dolls and stuffed animals. There was a television set in the corner and a few small chairs that sat under hanging pictures. For some odd reason, we decided to open her closet door. Much to our surprise and satisfaction we saw boxes of crackers, cereals and all types of canned foods, packed so tightly onto the closet shelves, that a few boxes actually fell to the floor when we cracked open the doors. Since we knew that we only had a small window to explore, we hurriedly picked up the boxes and replaced them on the shelves, closed the doors and moved along to the next room to take stock.

Tony's room was also chalk full of toys one might find in the average young American boy's bedroom. Cars and airplanes lined surfaces and sports posters adorned the walls. His bed was built to resemble a race car. Both children's beds, we noticed, were covered with heavy quilts and large, plush pillows. When we opened his closet doors, we found the same thing as in Michelle's room. His shelves were also overstuffed with food items. It was as if we'd discovered an oasis in the middle of a hot desert. Yet, we knew better than to take anything. There would most definitely be consequences should we disobey the lawmakers of this house. Our excitement fizzled at that realization. Even in our youth and inexperience, we knew the unspoken rules.

We went back to the kitchen and hastily washed our plates, then returned back downstairs to tell our younger brothers what we'd seen. When we returned back to our room, Steve pulled a box of crackers out from under his shirt.

"Hey you guys, come in here!" he shouted to the others. Though we knew better, we sat on our two small, single mattress beds and devoured the box of crackers as if they were the last fragments of food left on planet Earth. With our bellies no longer grumbling, we laughed for the first time since Ojai.

Not five minutes later, we heard the garage door go up and the car pull in, the sound of its brakes announced its arrival. Our jubilance evaporated in an instant and was replaced with fear and worry. As we heard our father's family head up the stairs, we quickly dispersed. The three youngest brothers went back to the television in the big room and Steve and I headed to our room. About fifteen minutes later, Lynn and our father thudded down the stairs and into the big room where Tim, Pat and Terry sat.

"Steve and Kevin, come in here now!" my father yelled angrily. As we walked into the room, his glare burned holes in each of us. Lynn stood next to him, her arms crossed in a defensive manner.

"Who went into my childrens' rooms?!" she shouted hysterically. Her anger shocked us. We had never seen her display such rage. This was the first time that we'd glimpsed the fury within her. It was a dark omen of things to come. "This will not be tolerated! You are forbidden to go upstairs at any time except when we give you permission! Is that understood?" she continued to shout.

"You kids are restricted to your rooms! I want your lights out by six! Have I made myself clear?!" Our father yelled next. Our voices, nothing but lumps in our throats, remained silent as we hung our heads and returned to our rooms.

"Kevin, we have to figure out a way to get out of this place. I'm not going to be able to live like this and neither are you," Steve said.

"What should we do? We have no place to go. Maybe if we somehow got back to

Ojai, Mom might take us back," I replied. Thoughts about escaping swirled in my head, overpowering the insistent, gnawing thoughts of hunger. At some point that evening, sleep overcame me.

The following morning, I realized that the only way to escape the cold was to take a shower. My brothers followed suit, and we all lined up in the hallway to wait our turn. While I waited in the drafty hallway, I poked my head into the laundry room where the freezer had been installed the previous day. I felt a bit daring, it came as a surprise even to me after the events of yesterday. I walked to the freezer and pulled open the door. What I saw made me want to shout with joy. Rushing back to my brothers I said giddily, "Hey guys, that freezer is loaded with meat! It's frozen, but it's there." They filed behind me back to the small laundry room, in anticipation to see the miracle. "We'll tell Steve when he gets out of the shower," I said. "What do you think Tim?" I asked, grinning. He looked apprehensive. For any of us to believe that what we'd found might benefit us, was a challenge.

"What's up guys?" asked Steve as he walked by the door, drying himself.

"Come take a look! Remember the freezer they put in yesterday?" I said, with a grin. Before he could come and see for himself, Lynn mysteriously appeared at the door.

"What are you guys looking for? This freezer is off-limits to you," she said firmly as she walked through us and into the laundry room. She then pulled a metal lock out of her pocket and slapped it on the freezer door with a smirk. Then she turned and breezed back past us towards the stairs without saying a word. I wasn't certain but I could have sworn I heard her singing as she climbed the stairs.

When I laid in bed that night, a sense of absolute helplessness came over me. Steve had the small radio playing that he'd found somewhere at school, it was tuned to a Portland station. While we both laid there listening, the song, *American Pie* played. It was the very same song that Steve had hummed the day that the minister showed up at our house. I lay there and gazed at the frost-covered window and puzzled about our fate.

9.

TWO WEEKS HAD passed since we'd discovered the food storage in Lynn's childrens' bedroom closets. Weight was quickly disappearing from my body as well as my brothers.' What was happening to us was conspicuous to anyone who paid attention, our withering physiques could no longer be hidden by our clothes. Fellow classmates were now offering food to me without my having to ask. One afternoon, I glanced across the packed cafeteria and Terry, who was engaged in conversation with one of his schoolmates, grabbed my attention. I noticed how his cheeks were sunken and how frail he appeared. He looked as if he had lost at least fifteen pounds during the short time we had lived here. It then sank in, that what I was looking at, was a stark reflection of myself, only without a mirror.

The principal of the school stood at the cafeteria door, his eyes swept across the room and stopped on me. He stared, fixated on me, for a solid three minutes. After what seemed like an uncomfortably long gawk, he strode across the crowded room, weaving his way through children, to where I was seated. "Hello, I'm Mr. Masterson the Principal. Do you have a moment? I would like to speak with you. It won't take very long," he leaned over and said to me. He then turned and walked away. He headed towards the cafeteria door, glancing briefly over his shoulder in my direction, as if to encourage me to follow. I got up and did so. At this, many students, including my own brother, watched with interest.

Once in the hallway, he walked by my side. He seemed genuinely interested in me, and his gestures suggested kindness. "How are you settling in here at Gardner?" he asked.

"It seems like a cool place," I replied. We'd reached the office door where his name was inscribed on a plaque below its window. He gestured to me as he spoke.

"Come on in and relax. This will only take a few minutes." I sat down in his relatively modest office and noticed a picture of his family sitting on his desk. He didn't waste any time. "Are things okay at home? I am interested in every student at this school."

I paused for a moment before responding. "I guess things are okay," I said with a degree of hesitation. I was reluctant to share about our current living situation, perhaps out of shame, or perhaps from the feeling that I was weak and incapable of dealing with the hardship that my brothers and I faced.

"I know your father and Lynn, and I would be happy to ask if there is anything I could do to help, if needed," he said in a very soft voice. My hair stood up on end as I listened to his offer. Sheer terror filled my entire body in that moment, and I felt as if I might panic. I tried to envision how my father and Lynn might respond to Mr. Masterson's offer, and I knew that things would not be good for us at home if we accepted any kind of outside intervention.

"I don't know," I sheepishly replied, trying to hide the fear in my voice. He could sense my uneasiness. He rose from his chair, walked around the desk and placed his hand on my shoulder.

"Everything will be alright, son. You can leave now." With that, he walked out into the hallway and began greeting students in his usual manner. I felt torn by my emotions. I was fearful that Dad and Lynn might find out about our conversation, but felt peace in knowing that there was at least one grownup out there that cared.

After school, Terry and I sat together on the bus. "Everyone thought you were in trouble, what did Mr. Masterson do?" asked Terry.

"He said he knows Dad and Lynn and wants to talk to them, or at least offer help."

"Help how? Dad will punish you if he thinks you told anyone what's going on at home!" he said with exasperation.

"I didn't say anything. Terry, we do need help. We can't keep living this way. I don't know what to do," I whimpered. At this point, we were the only two kids left on the bus and we both remained silent for the remainder of the trip back to Evergreen Drive.

When we got back to the house, Terry and I walked through the front door and into the chill of the first floor. Things were solemn and still as usual. We heard the faint noise of a television upstairs. "I wonder if we are going to get any dinner tonight?" Terry thought aloud. We parted and went to our separate rooms. I had just settled on my bed when our father rushed into my room. His face was twisted with anger and disgust towards me, as if he'd just witnessed me commit some horrific act of violence.

"I just spoke with Mr. Masterson! What have you been saying at school?! You kids are ruining my career goddammit! We are doing the best we can for you guys and this is how you repay us? Terry, get in here!" he shouted. "What are you two doing? Lynn is so angry with you both that she doesn't even want to see you!"

"I swear I didn't say anything," I said, as I shrank against the bedroom wall.

"I thought I taught you kids not to lie! Go to bed. You don't get any dinner tonight," he yelled, slamming the bedroom door as he left. Terry turned falteringly and drifted back to his room. His body posture was tense, as if he anticipated a forthcoming punishment.

Steve had not yet arrived home. I lit a candle that I'd found and turned on the small radio to provide me company and to ease the feeling of hopelessness. As I laid on my bed, I felt anguish and sorrow simultaneously. I was in a free fall and there was nothing below to catch me. I contemplated what mistakes, if any, I had made to deserve this life. I felt completely insignificant, like a grain of sand on a beach, tossed and battered by waves. My mind spiraled. Thoughts swam through my head, how were my brothers capable of coping? How did they show such strength? How long would they be able to endure? Each one of them possessed some nameless quality that helped them to survive. I questioned whether I had gotten it too? Whatever the quality, it proved to be necessary for survival and a valuable asset to one's character.

10.

IT WAS SATURDAY morning in March. Rain had begun to replace the falling snow. I woke early and languidly climbed the stairs in search of breakfast. The older of my brothers were still sleeping and the youngest sat in front of the television in the big room. Nearly all had given up looking for food. Nourishment in this house was an impossibility. I found some powdered milk and bread in the mostly bare refrigerator, it was enough to momentarily quell the hunger. Any attempt to communicate with Dad or Lynn about the food situation was like asking a politician not to lie, it was inconceivable. Our attempts were futile, desperate, useless. Lynn had developed a deep disdain for us, and it continued to grow as the days went on. Similarly, our father's resentment towards us also grew.

"You guys want to go outside and help me build a fort?" I asked my younger brothers after I'd given up on my brief breakfast foray.

"Yeah," Pat and Terry replied in unison. I tried to lighten the mood and desired to do something, anything, to forget about our situation. I was sick to death of hunger and trauma. One brief moment of peace, a bit of laughter, a smile, was all I was after. These things were welcomed, cherished. They were like a rescue vessel momentarily appearing on the horizon, giving hope to marooned, shipwrecked survivors.

It was drizzling steadily when we walked from the house down across the meadow and into the wet forest. Wind blew through the tree branches and water droplets sprayed and fell from above with each gust. Before we could find our base logs to start construction on our fort, we heard our father's voice.

"I want you kids to come up here." It was hard to tell his tone. He didn't seem angry, but he'd never been kind. His voice was indifferent. We haltingly left the woods, wondering what we were in for now. As we got closer to the house, I noticed that he was standing next to a little white goat. He held a rope in one hand, the other end was tied around the goat's neck.

"Chuck Carpenter gave this to us. I want you to tie it to that tree down there. We may be able to get some milk from it," he said, pointing to a tree on the edge of the meadow.

We led the timid little goat down to the tree that our father indicated, two brothers with the neck rope and I with my hands on its back.

The goat was naturally curious and inquisitive and it looked us over as it did its new surroundings, bleating along the way. I immediately felt empathy for the goat. Its piercing yellow eyes darted nervously as it tried to decide what to make of its new home. That same feeling was still fresh in my mind, the fear of a new place and the cold and damp discomfort was very familiar to me. After we tied it to the tree, we began scraping pine needles and leaves that were scattered about the ground into a pile of bedding for the goat. We wanted to do right by the goat, to give it a better welcome than we had had. About twenty minutes went by before we finally felt comfortable leaving our new friend. As we walked back to the house, it bleated and watched us go. For the first time since we arrived in Oregon, I felt an inkling of joy.

Hours passed and the rain kept coming down. I worried for the goat, shelterless and tied to that tree. The constant drizzle had soaked its fur and the immediate ground around it, with the movement of its anxious hooves, had turned the ground to mud. I felt responsible for my new friend and I yearned to protect the goat more than I desired to protect myself. Perhaps this newfound purpose was a distraction for me. Or perhaps I felt since I could do nothing about my own living conditions, that maybe I could do something to better the goat's circumstances.

I searched around the house for my father. I felt a new sense of strength, boldness and determination. I was set on asking him if I could move the goat to a better, more sheltered location. Instead of my father, I found Lynn. Instantly, I felt deflated. My first instinct was to retreat, but I told myself to stay calm. I did not want to give up.

"What do you want?" She was cleaning a spot on the rug and spoke sharply without looking up.

"Where's my dad?" I asked.

"I don't know where your father is right now. What do you want?" She demanded.

"I wanted to ask if we could put the goat in the garage where it can be warm?" I delicately inquired. She shook her head with an irritated sigh and gestured in a swatting motion for me to leave. I walked back to my room deflated. Then Pat rushed in from the garage.

"I found these carrots in the trash. Let's give them to the goat!" Admittedly, we were tempted to consume them ourselves. But, the desire to help what we considered to be a more underprivileged life than ours, overwhelmed our own urges and we decided to share Pat's great discovery with our bovidae friend.

Quickly, we ran from the back of the house and down to the edge of the meadow where the goat was quietly tied. It watched us intently as we rushed towards it, wagging his small tail as we approached. "Here you go," I said to it, holding out a carrot. It quickly devoured the limp root vegetable from my hand, and in a matter of seconds, the food was gone. It bleated as if to graciously say 'thank you.' The sky was an ominous, foreboding grey. More rain was on its way. We took off back to the house to beat the weather. The goat bleated continuously while we were in sight, as if begging us not to leave it. Once back in the house, Pat and I heard the sound of chamber music coming from upstairs. From the base of the stairs, I bravely requested to anyone within earshot, if I could come up.

"Yes, come on up." Father's voice replied. "What is it?"

"The goat seems quite uncomfortable out there and I don't think it likes being tied to that tree," I said once up the stairs.

"What do you suggest we do about it? There is no other place to put him." He was in a reclined position on the couch, reading the newest edition of *Time Magazine* and spoke without looking up.

"Can we at least put it in the garage at night?" I pleaded.

"Kevin, don't you have anything better to do? How about taking out the trash?" He asked while briefly glancing over the magazine.

I left the room and went back outside to lug the metal trash cans up the gravel drive. Before I could get to the end, it started to rain again. The slow drizzle quickly turned into a downpour. With the dense dark cloud cover, twilight rapidly bled into the familiar darkness I'd gotten so accustomed to. While laying in my small bed that night, I heard the distant maa-ing sounds from my new friend. It broke my heart to think of that lonely living being without shelter, exposed to the wind and rain and unforgiving elements. Eventually, the sound of the rain lulled me to sleep.

The next morning, the room felt even more damp and chilled than normal. I looked over towards Steve's bed, he was still asleep. He'd come home late, well after I'd fallen asleep. He'd made friends with some of his class-mates from school and began staying away from the house for longer and longer periods of time. I can't say that I blamed him. I hauled myself out of bed and put my feet onto the cold floor. As I pulled my pants on one leg at a time, I was reminded of my withering frame. Steve stirred. "How's it going?" I asked.

"Shitty!" he groaned sleepily. "I'm being punished for

coming home late last night and for bringing food into the house." I quickly looked around the room and saw an open box with half of a pizza sitting on the dresser top.

"Can I have some?!" I asked frantically.

"Sure," he replied. I'd already snatched a piece from the box and had it halfway devoured before I heard his answer. It was cold but absolutely delicious.

Our three younger brothers were huddled in their usual place in front of the T.V. when I told them about the pizza Steve had brought home. They leapt up and blazed down the hallway into our room, begging Steve to share the cold Italian delight with them.

Feeling more satiated than I ever had on powdered milk and dry bread, I went to the back door and slid open the glass. I stepped outside and headed down the slope to visit the goat. The ground was wet and littered with freshly fallen pine needles and big maple leaves from last night's rainfall. The goat was standing patiently. As I approached, it attempted to come towards me but was restrained by the rope that kept it bound to the tree. I stroked its wet fur and it nudged his head against me.

"I will move you into the garage," I quietly promised the goat. "I can tell you are not happy here. I'm so sorry."

"How is it doing!?" Pat shouted as he ran down to where we were.

"It's not happy. Look at how wet it is."

"I know."

"Let's take him up to the garage. We can make a bed for him," I suggested.

"Do you think dad will let us do that?"

"I don't know. Let's try it anyway. By the way, that pizza was good, huh?" I said. Pat's smile told me he whole-heartedly agreed.

As the day progressed and dusk set in, the sky cleared and faded to a soft blue. The wind started blowing and gently swept water droplets from the branches of the trees. My younger brothers and I led the goat up the wet slope to the house. When we opened the garage door, our friend was hesitant to enter. It took some coaxing but we were finally able to lead the goat, still dripping wet from the rainstorm into the corner of the garage where we'd made a makeshift stall. We'd piled old newspapers and a few small foot rugs together to make a liner. It maa-ed in its new, dry, more appealing environment. And it appeared to us to be more comfortable. The pungent odor of its wet fur permeated the garage. We laughed at the comical faces the goat made in inquisitiveness about its new surroundings. Then, it reached over and found an old pair of leather gloves hanging on the wall, lifted them off their hook and began chewing on them. Steve wasn't allowed out of our room in punishment for his late night, so I left our garage gathering to update him on what we were doing.

"What did Dad say?" was his immediate response. I was vague, but filled him in on our activities with the goat and the goals we were trying to accomplish.

"Thanks for helping it out. I felt sorry for it out there, all alone," Steve said.

"We found some carrots in the trash and gave them to it, but I wish we had more food to give it."

"Yeah. But what about finding food for us first?" he said sarcastically. "You guys finished off the rest of that pizza pretty quick!"

I left the room and went back to the garage to find Pat and Tim playing with the goat. Right when I arrived, so did Lynn. She'd entered the garage from the outside entrance, so none of us saw her coming. She said nothing, but her piercing stare burned holes in each and every one of us. Frozen, with her arms crossed in front of the chest of her turtleneck sweater, she finally screamed.

"Dick!" She quickly stomped off to find our father. "Dick! Dick!" she yelled repetitively. The calls reverberated off of the concrete floor, up the stairs and into the house. We stayed with the goat, soothing it, comforting it, in an attempt to prepare it for what we knew was to come. As expected, our father quickly appeared in the door to the garage, like a warrior ready for battle, chest broad, hands-on hips. His face was stone cold, emotionless.

"You kids get it out of here. Kevin, you don't listen well, do you?" he said, detached.

"You didn't tell me I couldn't bring it –" I hadn't had a chance to finish my sentence when he interrupted.

"When are you going to listen? Take it back outside." He stood motionless and watched us as we led the goat back out of the garage and down to the tree where he had been tied the night before. The goat was quiet as we led it, it was as if it knew to surrender. As we tied it back to the tree, my mind whirred with what I could do to make it more comfortable. I ran back to the house into my room and swept the one blanket I had off of my bed. "What are you doing?" Steve asked me as I headed for the back door. I said nothing.

When I got back to the goat, I draped my blanket over its wet back. It maa-ed quietly, as if to acknowledge the act of kindness from one living creature to another. The ground was still extremely wet and smelled of decaying leaves and pine needles. Between the odor of the goat and that of the fallen foliage, fresh rain and surrounding trees, I felt a sense of peace, of oneness. Little did I know, I was soon to be just like this goat, lonely, cold, and completely exposed to the elements.

11.

WITH ONLY MY jacket to cover me that night in bed, I gazed out of the window toward the dark night sky and waited for the familiar, faint sound of the goat's bleating, but it never came. The following morning we left early for school, and walked down that formidable, lonely street with only bread and powdered milk in our stomachs. While sitting, waiting in the small covered bus shelter, we reminisced about the warmth of Ojai and the orange orchards we used to play in during the summer months. Rain started to fall again from the grey sky above. Then, the headlights of the school bus cut through the darkness like a welcome searchlight.

Once again, we bumped over the dark, rural roads, and my mind wandered. I wondered what had happened to our now fragmented family, and why we hadn't heard from our mother or grandfather? When the bus stopped at Sherman's small rural intersection, I thought again about how his mother must care deeply for him. Everyday we watched as he struggled to climb the bus steps, his handicap preventing the fluid movements that most children simply took for granted. I then speculated whether or not his handicap was any more debilitating than that of the affliction of neglect? Perhaps Sherman had it pretty good after all.

When we got home from school that night, I immediately dropped my bag and ran down the sloped meadow to see my furry friend. The light was quickly fading. As I approached, I found it lying on its side. "Hey there, what are you doing?" I asked softly. It was motionless, the rope tied around its neck was now slack. Its yellow eyes were fixed skyward. "Do you want something to eat? I saved you a piece of bread," I asked, not quite understanding what I saw. My lip then stiffened and I found it difficult to catch my breath. I suddenly felt like there was a tremendous amount of weight pressing on my chest. I dropped to my knees and then turned to sit with the goat, my pants soaked the wetness from the earth. I sat motionless, my bare hand resting on the goat's still head.

"Please come back," I pleaded. "I'm sorry for not taking better care of you." As I sat, tears welling in my eyes, my mind swelled with the thought that all the goat wanted was companionship, food and shelter. This sweet creature had been denied its most basic needs. The last day of its life was spent in isolation, in loneliness. My body crumpled at that thought and tears began to spill. The sky went dark and the temperature dropped but I found myself numb to the black cold. I sat with my friend for hours, staring at the house, its borders bleeding into the surrounding darkness. I did not want to abandon my only friend. I needed to stay outside and be there with the goat.

"Please come back," I wailed, my sorrow unbearable. Hours passed before I stood up from its lifeless body. I slowly removed the wet blanket from its back and walked up the meadow towards the house with it draped over my shoulder. I tripped several times, unable to navigate the uneven terrain in the dark. When I reached the porch, I turned back toward where the goat lay. It was a dark, cold, and lonely place. Its wonderful maaing sounds would never be heard again. I bid my friend a final goodbye and opened the door to the house. I'd loved that goat.

In the house, I heard my father holler down the stairs, "I want you boys to bury that goat tomorrow! Now get to bed." His apathetic comment crushed me. It was a clear demonstration of a man whose love of family had unraveled into mere fibers of what once was, assuming he'd ever had it to begin with.

12.

IT WAS MONDAY morning. The Oregon landscape was in transition. Snow had already melted from the fields to behold wild grasses, long held in dormancy, just beginning to thrust their green shoots through the moist soil. Like the winter grasses, my brothers and I went into a sort of dormancy. After a period of time, adaptation became a means of survival for the five of us. Everything became relative, even the beauty of the spring landscape which temporarily nullified the hardships we were enduring at home, could not wake us from our abeyance. Our protective modes became our default way of being. To school and back again, day in and out, we simply stayed on autopilot.

On schedule that Monday in March, Sherman diligently waited at his bus stop for his morning ride. After clamoring laboriously up the stairs, he occupied his usual seat behind the driver. This particular morning, he turned around and peered over his shoulder directly at me. When we made eye contact, a smirk overcame the typical solemn expression that he wore for just one swift moment.

"Kevin, did you finish the math homework we were supposed to have done?" Howard asked from a few seats behind me.

"Not yet. I will probably get busted by Mr. Spilman for not having it completed," I replied.

"Me too," Howard agreed with a laugh.

As we emptied from the bus and I passed Sherman's seat, he looked up at me, smiled and asked, "Do you want to meet me at lunch in the cafeteria?"

"Sure. See you then," I responded.

The cafeteria was less crowded on these warm spring days. Most of the children preferred to be outside with the welcome change in the weather. When I got to lunch, I spotted Sherman sitting alone at the far end of one of the long plastic tables. "How's it going?" I asked.

He returned a greeting and as I sat, he slid his full lunch tray across the table towards me. There was something different about him, he seemed to possess wisdom far beyond his years. He made no eye contact with me as he spoke.

"There is a rumor going around that you are being tortured. My dog even weighs more than you do."

"Tortured?" I asked. "Nah, I guess I just don't understand some things. I don't really like it here, maybe that's it. I miss Ojai, that is where I came from. Thanks for the food. Are you sure you don't want it?" I chose not to tell him the truth for fear of the repercussions I might face.

"Where is Ojai?" he inquired as he raised his hand to brush away my thanks for the good.

"California," I said.

Mr. Masterson entered the cafeteria just then. His demeanor was always inviting. Though short in stature, he carried himself confidently and emitted a calm sense of authority. I felt that his good posture encouraged others to have a positive impression of him. His mouth was almost always turned up in a smile that lit up his face. As he approached Sherman and me at our lunch table, he casually greeted the students that he passed by with a warm grin.

"Hello Sherman. How is your mother? I know this is a hard time for you and your family. Please let me know if there is anything I can do." He then turned to me, "Kevin, may I speak to you for a moment?" I looked over at Sherman inquisitively, wondering what Mr. Masterson meant by what he'd said.

The principal and I moved to another table and sat away from the other kids. "Kevin, I have already spoken to your brother Terry. I think you both should speak to your father about seeking family counseling. These people are very good and work with a lot of families who are experiencing problems," he extended his hand with a card as he spoke. "Have a good day and please let me know if there is anything else I can do to help," he said as he rose from the table. I glanced over to where Sherman was sitting, but his chair was now empty.

Terry and I sat together on the bus ride home. "Mr Masterson said he talked to you. What do you think?" I asked Terry.

"I don't know Kev. Dad is not going to like it if we bring this up," he replied fearfully.

We sat in silence most of the way home, pondering what to do. Once we arrived at our stop and got out of earshot of others, we picked up our conversation about our current dilemma. One thing we agreed on was the fact that we didn't think we could endure our current living conditions for much longer.

"Do you ever wonder why we haven't heard from Mom?" I asked.

"She has probably tried to write to us, but since Lynn goes through the mail it is hard to really know," he said.

I'd replayed our last day in Ojai over and over again in my mind. Why had our mother completely dismissed us? Why didn't she desire to see us before we were sent away? It had been three months without any word from her, and that had had a tremendous emotional impact on all five of us, particularly the younger ones. Over the course of the last few months, I had developed a degree of distrust towards myself as well. My self-worth was fragile and all that had been said and done to us, had not only eroded my belief in others, but also my assurance of myself. I wondered if my life had any value?

So there we were, together, but completely alone. We took long slow steps down Evergreen Drive toward the house of living hell. When we reached the front door, we headed for the stairs and like every other day, into the ever increasingly empty kitchen.

"Let's see what we can find," I said to Terry as I headed to the refrigerator. There was half of a loaf of bread and a jar of mustard, that was the sum of all food to be found. Terry shook his head and turned to go back downstairs. I followed him, almost on his heels.

"I'm gonna call that number," I softly said to him.

"Kev don't! We're not supposed to use the phone," he nervously replied.

"Dad's not home yet. I'll make it quick," I said as I ran back up the stairs. I wanted assurance that no one was in close proximity so I remained silent, listening intently for any sounds before picking up the receiver. The dial tone was alarmingly loud. I dialed the number written on the card, and jumped when I realized that Terry was standing behind me. It was a gesture of moral support.

"Social Services, this is Agnes Marie. How may I help you?" I was speechless at first and found it difficult to form a sentence. "Hello? How can I help you?" she inquired again. Finally, my voice broke and I answered.

"Hello. My family is having problems and I was wondering if we could talk to someone?"

"Certainly. First, is this an emergency?" she asked.

"No," I quickly responded. "We just need someone to talk to."

"Most of our counselors have left for the day but I would be happy to have one of them return your call. What is your name and phone number?" I hesitantly relinquished the information.

"I'll have someone give you a call tomorrow. Are you sure everything is alright?" she asked again.

"Yes. Thank you," I turned to Terry and we both stared at one another. We knew this step would be one of significance, but to what degree, we were unsure. Our eyes did the speaking for us, no words were needed to express our thoughts. We'd finally done something to try and end the abuse.

The next day when I returned from school, I found Pat and Tim in their room sitting on their beds with the door wide open. I walked in slowly and asked how they were doing. Something was awry. Pat said Lynn threatened him in some way but he was vague. I asked what happened. "She pulled a knife on me," he said, fighting the urge to cry. He was nervous and obviously distraught.

"What?" I asked.

"I was upstairs looking for something to eat and she told me to go back downstairs. I saw a letter from mom to us laying on the counter and reached for it. She told me to leave it alone but I took it. She yelled at me to drop it. She was holding a knife," he said, still visibly shaken. It was then I knew, without a shadow of a doubt, that Lynn had been withholding our mail.

"Terry and I called social services last night and I asked if we could talk to someone about all of this. They're supposed to call back. I don't know what will happen but I think we might get some help, at least I hope so," I said.

It was about six-thirty in the evening. I was in my room alone and had removed the small pipe I'd found in Ventura, left by the old Mexican man, from the dresser drawer and held it. In a way, holding it took me back. It was a way for me to recollect the place where I had come from, and to mentally remove myself from my current environment. I stared at the smooth, worn surface that spoke of its history as I rolled it to and fro in my palm.

All of the sudden, my father burst through my bedroom door. His face was an unnatural red color. His expression was stern, like a composer, fixed and unmovable. I knew right away that I was in trouble.

"Did you call social services, goddammit!?" he yelled as he strode towards me. Before I could answer, he continued. "Number one, you are not to use the phone without our permission! Number two, are you trying to ruin my career? First your principal and now this!"

"I just want to talk about things. I want to find a way where we can all agree," I said cautiously.

"We took you in as a way to help your mother. You boys have been nothing but trouble since you arrived. Tim has been the only one who has been easy to deal with," he said. By now, Terry and Pat stood in the doorway, listening with frightened intent.

"Isn't there a way we can at least just talk to a counselor?" I asked.

"Goddammit, Kevin! I'm going to blow my stack! We are not going to talk with any counselor and you are not going to reach out to any of these people ever again. Have I made myself clear?" he shouted as he walked from the room.

Terry came in and told me he knew this would happen and slowly backed out of the room. Steve, who had joined the basketball team at school to stay away as long as possible, had not yet come home. So I sat alone in our room. With the pipe still in my hand, I gazed out of the window and thought about the small town of Ojai that seemed so far away.

13.

MAY FINALLY ROLLED in but the nights in the basement were still quite cold. School had become a haven for me. It was the only way out of the dank chill of the concrete cell of our room. The bus ride to and from campus provided me time to reflect. And as time went on, I made up my mind, I was convicted to leave the situation I was in. I became determined to return back to the only place I had ever really felt comfortable, to the only place I had ever really known. How I was going to get back to California, I did not know. But I was determined to make it happen. It was a life or death situation, and I had faith that something would work out.

As the season continued to change and spring became summer, there was more warmth and sunlight than we'd seen in months. My walks down Evergreen Drive allowed me to observe the Northwest sunsets and I began to appreciate the natural beauty of the area. The street came alive, bustling with activity. There were people in their yards that I'd never set eyes on before and dogs that frolicked and played. One afternoon on my way home from the bus stop, I came up the gravel drive and found Pat sitting on the front step of the house. He was crying and holding his left arm.

"What's wrong?" I asked.

"I drove a nail into my hand. It really hurts a lot," he managed to say between his tears. His left hand lay open in his lap. At first, it appeared to be deformed, but I quickly realized that the deformity was due to swelling. He was in so much pain that I instantly knew he needed to see a doctor.

"Has anyone looked at it? Have you been to a doctor?" I asked.

"No. I went into Lynn's room and told her what happened. She said she didn't have time to take me to a doctor and to wait for Dad to come home. That's what I am doing, waiting for Dad."

I was stunned but not surprised. I got up, stepped over Pat and went into the house. I could hear someone banging around in the laundry room, opening and closing the washer and dryer doors. I went straight there and peaked inside, Lynn was aggressively throwing clothes into a laundry basket.

"Has anyone called a doctor for Pat?" I asked as I entered the room.

"He'll have to wait until your father comes home. I don't have time to deal with it,"

she replied without stopping what she was doing. I stood there, nervously fidgeting with the lock on the freezer, trying to come up with the right words to say to her. Before I could come up with anything, Lynn spun toward me, extending her right arm in my direction. In her hand was a small paring knife. She gripped it so tightly that her knuckles turned white and her hand trembled.

"Get away from that freezer! I'm sick and tired of you kids trying to get into it!" she shouted. I was shocked but not afraid.

"Don't smile at me!" she yelled, as if I were ten feet away from her instead of two.

I did not realize I was smiling in that moment, but her observation was correct. A lightbulb had gone off in my head. There was nothing more she could take away from me. There had been no food, attention, comfort, freedoms, or the ability to communicate with anyone, including our own mother. My heart had hardened towards her, I was impervious to her abuse. Surprisingly, I was able to stay calm and focused and say my piece.

"Pat's hand needs attention. I think it is important to get him to the doctor," I said with ease and confidence. She struck me on the shoulder with her left hand. It was more of a slap than a closed fisted blow. I did not respond but instead, turned and walked away. I returned to Pat on the front steps, sat down next to him and told him that our father should be home soon. Then my mind went someplace else. How can we leave this place, I wondered to myself. I looked back over my shoulder at the house. A cloud of sadness seemed to seep out of its walls. I felt sympathy for the structure, like I had the goat. And I could relate to its inability to influence what was happening to it.

The Volkswagen finally appeared from around the corner, moving slowly until it came to rest. My father opened the window and asked Pat to get in. He was nonchalant about it all, as if Pat had more of a scratch than a serious injury. This was yet another incident that was indicative of the level of care we received in the months of life with Dad and Lynn. They were dismissive of us, utterly unconcerned with our wellbeing.

It was ten o'clock that night before our father returned with Pat. Steve and I were in our room, engaged in idle banter, when we heard the sound of the Volkswagen pull into the garage. The atmosphere was silent except for the sound of the opening garage door on its tracks. Steve and I hopped up from our beds and went to see how Pat was doing. He walked slowly to the door of his room, with a newly bandaged hand hanging awkwardly at his side. We followed him into his bedroom and asked what the doctor had said.

"It was punctured and I had to have a tetanus shot," he said, his spirits lifted.

"Does it hurt much?" Steve asked.

"It did until they gave me something for the pain. It hurt so bad sitting out there waiting for Dad. The doctor was mad at Dad for waiting so long to get me in," he said. Staying true to form, Pat didn't make much of a fuss about his accident. He was stoic. He'd accepted his injury like he'd accepted our living conditions. On the verge of starvation, through abuse and neglect, he did not complain. I imagine Buddhist monks have the same disposition as Pat. And I hoped that somewhere deep inside me, I too possessed that same quality.

14.

THE NEXT DAY at noon, the school bell rang for lunch. Now, nearly all of the kids ate outside either on the bleachers or splayed out in the grass. Over the course of the last few months, I'd made friends with several other classmates, two of whom were seated together at the end of the football field. Brian saw me and signaled for me to join them.

"Hey Brian, Ed. What's going on?" I asked.

"Just hanging out. Why don't you sit down with us?" Brian retorted. So I did. Approximately ten minutes passed before I said anything. They were talking about their fathers and how they'd found old coins using a metal detector someplace on the far eastside of Portland.

"What kind of coins?" I interjected.

"I'm not sure. I saw a few that they found and they look old is all. I want them to take me along the next time they go and find some for myself," Brian said.

I had nothing to contribute to the conversation, but thought of the bottle I'd found at the bus stop where the old Mexican man had been sitting. I casually mentioned it and Ed turned toward me with interest.

"Tell me about it? What does it look like?" he asked. I described it in as much detail as I could. With as many times as I'd passed it through my hands, I knew every curve of glass that made up that little bottle.

"My dad collects old bottles. He may want to buy it from you if you would be interested in selling it? It also may be worth nothing and he may not want it," he replied. "Either way, why don't you bring it to school with you and I'll take it to him."

Initially, I did not want to sell it. But as I took in Ed's words, and thought about the possibility of the bottle's worth, my mind began to race with excitement. I was like an anxious child poised to unwrap a special gift on Christmas day. The desire I had to leave my current situation and return to Ojai was so strong that my thoughts started spinning. I imagined every possible mode of transportation, that the bottle might afford me, to get me back to the small valley. Perhaps this was the answer I'd been searching for.

"Sure, I'll bring it in tomorrow," I said, trying to conceal my excitement.

That night, I held the bottle in my hands and gazed at it with wonder and gratitude. In many ways, it kept me linked to the past. It had allowed me to remember a time and place much more pleasant than the present. It had served as a devotional item of sorts. It encouraged me to think peaceful thoughts, and create a kind of harmony in my mind. The bottle was embossed with the name "Reghetti." Who was he, I wondered? Could he have been a man devoted to his wife and family? Had the man at the bus stop left it for me on purpose? Was he clairvoyant? Or was he an old mystic, silent in speech but strong in unknown powers? If the bottle was worth my fare to Ojai, I wondered if I would ever meet the man again? My mind whirred. Was this bottle my lifeline?

As I rode the bus to school the next morning, I firmly grasped the bottle between my hands. I glanced up front to see if Sherman was in his usual seat. He was. There was an air of permanence about him. He was quiet, yet self-assured. As I thought about leaving, I wondered if he would remain in Clackamas County for the rest of his life?

The hallways were busy but when I bumped into Ed before lunch, I told him that I'd brought the bottle. He was preoccupied then, but told me to meet him outside for lunch. The warmer weather was inviting when I took my tray from the lunchroom outside to find Ed. He was laying on his back in the grass, soaking in the spring sunshine near a row of fir trees which lined the school property.

"Here it is," I said as I sat down next to him.

"What do you think of Wendy? Do you think she's a fox?" he said, ignoring the bottle.

"Yeah. But she's a bit stuck up, don't you think?" I replied.

"Yeah. You're right, but I still want to ask her out," he said with a smirk. Then, he took the bottle and dropped it in the grass next to him without even looking at it. At first, I felt a little bit snubbed. I was protective of the few personal items I had, and I didn't care much for the way he casually tossed it on the ground. He assured me he wouldn't break it and would show it to his dad when he got home. After a relatively insignificant conversation, the bell rang for class and we went our separate ways across the brown grass that just barely masked the fresh green shoots beneath our feet.

One week passed and there was still no word from Ed. I had not seen much of him at school and when I did, he was always preoccupied in small talk with other kids. Late one afternoon in between classes, I heard fast-paced footsteps echo down the hallway coming from behind.

"Kevin, my dad wants your bottle! He asked me to give you this check and said this is what he'll give you for it." We stood there in proud silence, as if we'd just made the deal of the century. His face broke into a grin, "Well, I gotta go. See you around!" he yelled mid-sprint down the hallway. I looked down at the check. It was made out to Kevin, with no last name, for the amount of forty-five dollars. My spirit soared. I was now confident that getting back to Ojai was not just a pipe dream. With restored hope, all I needed now was a plan on how to utilize the money to get there.

There was a small convenience store about two blocks from the school. Kids usually gathered there on class breaks. The clerk appeared to have adapted with great patience, to the chaos of droves of obnoxious teenagers. A solitary payphone sat outside of the store's front entrance and was the only means of communication for Terry or me to contact California. Most times, our attempt to reach our friends back home fell short. At that time, the location and condition of our mother was still unknown. Perhaps there were clues in the snail mail that could have led us back to mom, but Lynn stood in the way of that.

I searched through a ragged phone book that hung underneath the phone and found the telephone number for the Greyhound bus station. I dialed the number.

"Greyhound Bus Services, this is Christine, how may I help you?"

"How much is a ticket from Portland to Ventura?" I asked nervously.

"On what date and is this to be one way?" she questioned. I quickly shuffled through dates in my head trying to determine the last day of school before summer vacation. "Hello, are you there"? she inquired.

"June 6th please," I replied, taking a stab at the date.

"Please hold on."

As I waited for her I thought about leaving my brothers, and a sinking feeling came over me. I felt as if I was abandoning them and then I felt an unexplainable guilt. Shockingly, the feeling that came over me next was a feeling of compassion for my father. I wondered what had happened in his life that would have caused him to be such an unhappy individual? He was a teacher that got to play an instrumental role in the lives of many children, wouldn't that be a tremendously rewarding experience, I wondered. He had worked hard to obtain a PhD in teaching, and had brought five good boys into the world in the process. What went wrong?

"That will be thirty-eight dollars. Would you like to purchase the ticket now?" she asked.

"No, I'll try to come there and buy it this weekend. Thanks," I responded.

My dream of leaving Evergreen Drive was coming to fruition. The thought of where I would stay when I actually got to Ojai did occur to me, but I brushed it off. The security I felt in leaving, prevailed over the fear of the unknown.

That afternoon, when I stepped back onto the bus to Evergreen Drive, I stopped at Sherman's seat and asked if I could join him. He enthusiastically agreed. For the first time, I felt comfortable confiding in someone. I was ready to share my secret plans with a friend. He listened intently as I rattled on for a solid five minutes, and then he asked very simply, "Where will you stay?"

"I don't know yet. I guess I'll start looking for friends. Maybe my mom will allow me to live with her," I said.

There was a long pause and then, with a look of hurt, Sherman said, "It has been nice knowing you. But I have one question, you don't treat me like the others, why is that?"

"Because I think you are a good guy. Do you want to come along?" I smiled sheepishly as I asked.

15.

IT WAS EARLY one morning in June. Steve and I headed down through a heavily vegetated area behind the house on Evergreen Drive to a small body of water which we'd coined 'Mint Lake.' The heaviness of the humidity was stifling and noisy swarms of mosquitoes hung like dense curtains in the air. The forest was thick and fragrant. We walked silently except for the occasional crackling of branches breaking beneath our feet. In the far distance, we heard the muffled sound of a chainsaw, likely a neighbor cleaning up their property. The sun's rays glistened through the treetops and illuminated buzzing insects as they traveled in and out of the beams. Steve reached for a broken branch and used it to clear spider webs and foliage along our makeshift path. Early morning dew lingered on the leaves of the perennial plants snuggled beneath the pines.

"When are you planning on leaving?" Steve asked as he stooped to clear a fallen branch.

"When I find a ride to the bus station. I think I can cash the check at a bank and then I will buy the ticket and hopefully leave the same day." I said as I swept insects away from my face. " I feel bad leaving you guys."

"Don't worry about us. Do whatever you can to get out of here," Steve replied.

"I'll do what I can to get you guys out of here as well," I offered.

We continued to trailblaze through the woods and found ourselves in a dense area of forest that was unrecognizable. We both stopped to collect our bearings. As we stood there in stillness, we faintly heard what sounded like Terry or Pat yelling from the direction of the house.

"Let's go back. Something is going on," Steve said with

a sigh. We retraced our route and fifteen minutes later, emerged into the meadow behind the house. Everything was quiet as we crossed the meadow and went up to the back door. When I reached for the handle to slide it open, I heard Terry whispering yelling from the left side of the house. I stopped and looked in his direction, he was gesturing for us to come to where he stood.

"What is going on?" Steve asked.

"I'm so pissed. You guys will be too when you find out," Terry said in a subdued voice. "Lynn just went through our rooms and threw all of our stuff in the trash."

"All of it!?" I exclaimed, feeling a sense of panic rise in my chest.

"I think so but I'm not sure. I'm so pissed. I'm out of here!" Terry replied.

"Do you have a place to go if you do decide to leave?" I asked. Terry lowered his voice, as if he knew someone was listening.

"Carl said I could stay with him at his house. I think what I'm –" He stopped mid-sentence as the sliding glass door opened. Our backs were turned to it but Terry watched the door intently. He exhaled and relaxed, "It's just Pat." I turned around as Pat walked towards us, visibly upset.

"Lynn threw my stuff away. Even my comics!" he said, sounding browbeaten. Steve and I had yet to look into our room. We went to the door and as we entered, we heard low voices coming from upstairs. There was an intense odor, not usually present inside the house, that seemed to be emanating from every direction.

"What is that smell?" I asked. I followed Steve down the hallway to our bedroom. When he opened the door, we were hit in the face by a horrible stench. Steve gasped, stepped back into the hallway and quickly slammed the bedroom door.

The odor had a chemical smell and reeked of ammonia. Braving the stench, we held our breath and entered the room to find that most of our things had been taken as well. The room had been thoroughly bleached and disinfected. My burning eyes swept the mostly vacant room until I saw my small yellow pipe still sitting in the window sill where I'd left it. At least it had not been discarded. Steve and I locked eyes momentarily and then sprinted for the door, gasping for air. He was visibly angered and I'd hit my limit. It was time to leave this place.

I was intimidated and felt trepidation in regards to informing my father about my desire to leave. But I had to tell him to avoid the possibility that someone might notify the authorities when I went missing. In my mind, I knew that he and Lynn would be relieved. One less burden to take care of, one less mouth to feed. It should come as a welcome surprise to them both, I thought. Still, I needed a guarantee that my break for it would not be in vain.

The house began to look different to me in many ways as I retraced my steps through the hallway and headed up the stairs. Once I'd ascended, I announced myself and sought the permission that I had become so accustomed to, before I entered through the door. My father sat on the deck outside and gave a shout to acknowledge my presence.

"Come on up!" He was occupied with the newspaper, and his eyes remained lowered on it as he spoke. "Lynn said she took the liberty of cleaning your rooms for you and that they were an absolute mess."

"She took most of our stuff. I'm going to look through the trash and see if I can get anything back," I said somewhat defensively.

"Leave it! I'm sure she wouldn't throw anything away that was important to you kids," he replied.

"I want to visit my friends in Ojai for the summer," the words sprang unexpectedly from my mouth.

"Really? How do you plan to do that?" he asked, still staring at the newspaper.

"I sold that bottle that I had, and I want to buy a bus ticket with the money that I got from it," I said apprehensively.

"Okay," he said. I was taken back by his casual response. I hesitated, waiting for more, but he said nothing. Then I noticed smoke drifting up from the neighbor's burning woodpile. It moved gradually to the east in silence. Its destination was unknown. Briefly, I was captivated by its movement, by its sense of freedom.

My father looked up from his paper. "I'll tell you what, if you promise to come back, I'll take you to the bus station. But first, I want to tell you a few things. Lynn has gone out of her way to take you kids in, and take care of you. You have not respected her at all while you've been here. I want you to put yourself in her shoes. Imagine if you received a notice from a minister that you didn't know, which told you that you were going to have five kids dropped in your lap. Can you blame her for being frustrated?" he asked. Before I could reply, he dropped his eyes back to his newspaper. "When are you planning to leave?"

"Thanks. I checked with the Greyhound schedule and there is a bus leaving at 10:15 Friday morning. Can you take me then?" I asked.

"You know, I really don't care, Kevin," he replied sharply. The sting of his words dampened my excitement but I kept my chin up as I turned to walk away.

Friday morning arrived and it took only a matter of minutes to pack my possessions. I removed the small pipe from the sill where it had rested for the past five months, and placed it in my pocket. I then went to Steve's bed where he was still sleeping. "Steve, I'm leaving," I said quietly.

"Hey, take care of yourself. Try to connect with Sam Jensen or Kevin Small when you get to Ojai. They may be able to help you if you can't find Mom. I'll try to catch up with you when I get down there," he said as he rubbed sleep from his eyes.

"Take it easy," I said and walked out of the door. I then peaked into our brothers' room. "Hey guys, I'm leaving."

"Take care Kev," Terry said. Then I heard Pat's voice.

"See you."

"We're glad for you, " said Tim.

"I'll see what I can do to help you guys," I spoke softly, I did not want to be overheard.

Then our father shouted from the garage, "Let's go! I have to be back here by one o'clock!" As I headed for the car, Lynn met us at the door.

"You know he's going to stay down there. Why are you doing this Dick?" she asked my father with folded arms.

"He promised he would come back," he said to her as he climbed into the driver's seat. She threw her arms in the air and turned away in frustration. As we slowly backed out of the garage, I looked at that sad little house for the final time.

There was little said in the car, so I watched the tree-lined meadows pass by the window one after another, like I'd done on the school bus so many times before. I recollected the first time I'd seen them five months ago, cloaked in darkness, when my brother's and I had arrived in this strange place.

"Where are you going to stay?" asked my father over the familiar whine of the old car engine.

"There are a few people I can stay with. Sam and Kevin, who are Steve's friends, might be an option for me. If I find where Mom is now, I might be able to stay with her," I replied.

"Your mother's last address was on the letter she sent you kids," he said.

"What letter? I never saw any letter from mom," I exclaimed in surprise. "She sent a letter?"

"Don't start that again! Lynn gave all of those letters to you kids. Why you have never given her a chance is beyond me for Pete's sake! Do you know there have been times when I have found her upstairs crying. You boys have made her life a living hell goddammit!" he shouted as he drove through a rural stop.

I racked my brain trying to remember whether we'd gotten a single letter since we'd arrived in Portland. The only one I could think of had been sent to us by our grandfather from my father's side. It was a surprising dialogue on how we needed to respect our father and his wife. Evidently, we were "making things rough on them and we needed to behave ourselves." It was crystal clear that Lynn and Dad had given our grandfather an entirely different version of what was actually occurring under their roof.

I did not want to challenge his conviction about Lynn, or point out that we had never in fact, received any letters from our mother. But his words brought hope in the newfound knowledge that she had been trying to communicate with her children after all. I then began to wonder. If she'd been trying to reach us, and had never received a response, was she worried? Confused? Did she think that we didn't care or that we didn't want to hear from her ever again? The realization that she did actually care brought up a host of feelings that I had not felt in months. I wished that I could reach out to my brothers at that moment with the news.

As we approached Portland, forests and rural meadows turned to tract homes and bustling strip malls. "Can we stop at a bank? I need to cash this check," I asked as I fished it from my pocket. Dad nodded and pulled into the nearest one. I quickly went in and asked for cash. As the bank teller handed it over the counter to me, I felt instant gratitude for the old man who had left the little bottle behind on the bus station bench. And I wondered how he would feel if he knew that what he had given me, either inadvertently or deliberately, had helped me escape an abusive situation.

When we pulled in front of the station, I felt that I had come full circle. "The first thing I saw when I picked you guys up here back in December was five hungry and dirty boys. You promised you would come back, remember. This is why I'm letting you go," he said, looking me directly in the eyes.

"I will," I said, knowing that I wouldn't, and with no remorse for telling a bald-faced lie.

I walked through the doors and into the cigarette smoke-filled bus station. Without turning back, I listened to the whine of the Volkswagen engine echo through the lobby as my father pulled away. Perhaps it was the car's way of saying goodbye. An hour later, I sat in an aisle seat on the bus destined for Ventura, without a clue what I would do when I got there. I was at the mercy of the wind, like the smoke from the woodpile fire, and the litter from the bus stop parking lot, I was at the mercy of the wind.

PART 3
Grand Avenue, Ventura County California

16.

EARLY SATURDAY MORNING, I awoke briefly from the arduous night spent on the Greyhound by the sun rising above farm fields of the coastal plains of California. Most of the fields were brown, a dramatic contrast from the greenery I'd just left behind in northern Oregon. The allowance of time on the bus journey allowed me to reflect on what I'd experienced over the last five months. My mind drifted sleepily through memories until the occasional cough or muffled exchange of conversation brought me back to reality. I felt the heat of early summer seeping through the window from the dry landscape beyond. Captivated by the possibility of a new life, one with nourishment and void of abuse, I was lulled back to sleep.

I awoke again as the bus entered the outskirts of Santa Barbara. I was comforted by the sight of the pacific coast. One of the passengers sat with a small radio in her lap. The song *Ventura Highway* softly spilled from it and filled the bus. I gazed back out the window at the bleached white sand along the beach and became enamored by the summer sun. Reality finally set in, I had made it back. I was home in California, far far away from the house on Evergreen Drive.

When the bus eventually pulled into the Ventura station, I stepped down onto the cement sidewalk where I'd stood just five months ago, and was hit by a wave of emotion. I looked around for the bench where my brothers had sat to wait for our departing bus back in December. I missed them already. The bench where the old Mexican man had sat was now occupied by two young boys who were wrestling over a single box of candy. Again, my imagination took off. I speculated about where he'd gone, where he lived. And then I thought about how the things he'd left behind had provided me the means to stand where I was in that exact moment. I reached into my pocket for the pipe he'd left on that bench and immediately felt a connection to him. I kept my hand wrapped around the pipe as I stood there, contemplating how I was going to get to Ojai.

It was much warmer than it had been back in December, and the overall feeling of the place seemed to have changed since I'd been there last. It was no longer the place of my youth, but now rather, one of adulthood. The innocence I'd once felt had evaporated. I was alone and in survival mode. I walked down the sidewalk away from the bus station until I came to a blue street sign that just so happened to designate a stop for a bus service to Ojai. I stopped and felt the need to readjust both mentally and physically to the newness of this place. Salt air permeated everything and the fragrance of blooming flowers that were along the sidewalk over-loaded my senses. Everything was in stark contrast to the wet and woody environment I'd just left. An hour passed before the transit bus to Ojai arrived at the curb-side pick-up point. During that time, I racked my brain thinking about how I could contact my mother and friends.

I had just enough money to pay for the fare for the short transit ride to Ojai. The temperature changed dra-matically from cool coastline to warm inland weather. I'd brought very little when I left Oregon, save for the Pen-dleton wool blanket which I thought I might need, but it became evident that it was unnecessary at this time of year. It was two-thirty in the afternoon when the transit bus reached its final stop at Ojai's historic post office. The temperature registered 103°F. As I walked past the building's boundary, the stucco walls reflected the bright afternoon sunlight, intensifying the heat. Where to start, I wondered to myself. I could look for my high school friend, Jules. I knew where he lived and I figured that I could walk there in half an hour's time. The oak-lined streets were busy with traffic and pedestrians, even in the oppressive heat, and I had a hard time adjusting to the dramatic difference in temperature between Clacka-mas and Ventura counties.

It took me approximately thirty minutes to reach Jules' house. I stepped up to the front door and knocked. There was no answer. I'd have to go to plan B, I thought.

Before my mother's admittance to the hospital, she had worked as a teacher's assistant at the Monica Ross Preschool, nestled under a grove of big old oak trees on the east end of the valley, about five miles away. Exhausted from the heat, I decided to try and hitchhike. Car after car passed me by until finally, a white Chevy pickup stopped and the young man driving stuck his head out of the window.

"Where you going?" he asked.

"Gridley Road," I replied.

"Climb in."

I opened the door and peered into the cluttered cab, which smelled of motor oil and immediately recognized the driver. "George?" I asked. His hair was longer than I had remembered and his face was covered with a short bristly beard. He wore a flamboyant tropical shirt and white shorts.

"Kevin? Is that you? How have you been? We were wondering what happened to you guys! No news is not always good news," he said. George Gonzalez was the family counselor who had been assigned to our family for the few months between Dad's leaving and Mom's mental break when we lived on Mallory Way. He'd acted as the intermediate between the social service programs and my family. His job had been to assure that we received assistance, such as food stamps, during the time that our mother struggled to support us while on her own.

"I've been better. I just arrived a few hours ago from Oregon and I don't want to go back. It was rough. In fact, I will *not* go back there George," I stated firmly.

"What about Steve and your other brothers?" he inquired.

"They are still in Oregon. I felt bad leaving them, but I think Steve is leaving soon to come down, maybe today? Do you know where my mom is?" I asked hopefully.

"Yeah. I keep in touch with her and she asks about you guys all of the time. She's worried because she hasn't heard anything from you. She lives over on Country Club Drive in a small apartment. I would be happy to take you there. Where are you staying now?" he asked.

"Yes, please. I have nowhere to stay at the moment. I'm really glad you stopped," I said with a sigh of relief.

"You can crash at my place for a few days if you need to, but for only a few days. I can't have you longer than that," he said.

"Thank you, George, but I'll figure it out," I replied. I appreciated his offer but did not want to be an inconvenience to him or his family.

As we drove to where my mother lived, the summer heat intensified in conjunction with the odor in the cab. The glaring brightness of the sun's reflection off of walls and walks, was intense on my eyes, even though they'd thirsted to see these sights for quite some time. We pulled into the small parking lot in front of an apartment complex and George pointed to the door of my mother's apartment. I looked at the turquoise door with two small shrubs on either side, and I considered the past five months. What had mom been doing all this time? Everything was so different in Ojai now. Would my mom show obvious changes as well?

"Do you want to come in?" I asked George

"No. I gotta run. I'll see you around," he said as he put the pickup in reverse. He then gave a little wave as he pulled out of the parking lot.

I was apprehensive to approach the door, afraid of how my mother would react when she saw me. Slowly, I walked up and knocked, there was no answer. So I knocked again, still no answer. I considered the fact that there was nowhere else for me to go, so I sat and waited. While I sat there, nervous and exhausted, I felt a glimmer of hope. I was grateful to be home again, soaking in the mountain views, inhaling the fragrance of the eucalyptus trees, and breathing in the salt air. I basked in the sunshine, absorbing Ojai with all of my senses.

It was four o'clock in the afternoon when the yellow Ford Fairlane station wagon finally pulled into the parking lot. I was actually a little shocked that it still ran. Mom stepped from the car, not noticing me at first. She looked rested, and her blond hair was lighter than I remembered. "Mom!" I called out to her. She spun with a look of surprise.

"Kevin! For heaven's sake, where did you come from? I've been so worried about you boys! My word, how did you get here? Where are the others? Are you alone?"

"I took the bus. They're all still up there. I came alone. Let me help you with those things," I said as I reached for a bag of groceries. She took the apartment key from her purse and asked me to come inside. "How are you doing mom?' I asked with genuine concern.

"Ugh! It's been tough!" she exclaimed. "Sit down."

The rumbling of the air conditioner dampened the traffic noise outside. The coolness of the room was an immediate relief as I placed her groceries on the counter and sat in the small living room. The apartment was modestly furnished with a few things that I remembered from our old home on Mallory Way. The chair I sat in was one of those things.

"Tell me, how have you been? You look very thin Kevin. I've written to you boys numerous times and have never received a response. As you know, I will not speak to your father," she said.

"It's been rough, mom. Lynn did not treat us very well and dad pretty much let her do things that were not cool. Dad asked me to promise him that I would come back, so I told him I would, but I am not going back there. It's really bad," I took a deep breath, "Is there a chance I can stay here? I have no place else to go."

"Well, you can stay for a few days but I can't have you here any longer than that. If the welfare department finds you are staying with me, they could remove my assistance," she said relatively sternly.

She seemed happy to see me but acted a bit inconvenienced that I was there. It was at that moment that I knew I would have to find someplace else to go. I look back on that time now and wonder why my mom acted that way toward me. I know that she had been frustrated with her life's circumstances. Perhaps I was a reminder that she'd failed as a wife and mother. Or perhaps she was not yet mentally capable of caring for anyone other than herself. I don't think I will ever know. What I did know though, was that I was not welcome and that she was unwilling both emotionally and financially to have any of her children live with her at that time.

I slept on mom's living room floor for a few nights. During the day, I was occupied with searching for another place to live. After a few more unsuccessful attempts to catch up with Jules, I finally caught him at home one afternoon.

"Wow! Hey buddy! What are you doing here?" he asked with surprise.

"I had to get away from Oregon. Anyway, what have you been doing?" I asked gleefully.

"I left school and I'm at the Chaparral Teaching Center. I couldn't handle Nordhoff High anymore. Hey, by the way, I just bought a cool truck and have my driver's permit now. Do you want to cruise around for a while?" he asked, as he walked over to a beat-up white Ford pickup parked on the street curb. "Isn't it cool!? Look at these tires," he exclaimed with enthusiasm.

"Sure," I said, and we both climbed in. The black leather seat was hot from the afternoon sun and the floorboard was nearly rusted away.

"It's a little tricky to start but it will kick over here in a bit," he said as he repeatedly turned the key. After a few tries, the engine stubbornly grumbled to life, belching plumes of exhaust that blackened the surroundings. He lightheartedly revved the engine and shouted over the noise, "Let's cruise up to the east end and around the orchards!"

When we passed the tract homes that I used to ride my bike by as a young kid, I felt my emotions welling up. I longed for that time when we were all together as a family, and I couldn't fathom how it had all been lost. Family, to me, was an elusive notion. To hold on to people was like trying to grasp a handful of sand. No matter what I did, or how hard I tried to hold on, I could not keep the grains of a family from slipping through my fingertips.

After riding in the truck for a while, I finally mustered the nerve to pop the question. "Is there a chance I can crash at your house for a while?" I asked Jules bluntly.

"What? I can't hear you!" he shouted over the obnoxiously loud motor. I repeated my question, this time yelling.

"Nah, I don't think my mom would let us do that! She likes you and everything but she's pretty particular about the house. She wants me to get out pretty soon as well!" he shouted back.

Apart from the engine noise, we sat in silence as we traversed the back roads that served the citrus orchards. Long walls of stacked river rock delineated the orchards.

The fragrance of blossoming citrus trees sweetened the warm air. I found it pleasant, as overwhelmed as I was at the time. The orchard trees were planted in straight rows, their dramatic canopies shaded the ground beneath. As I watched the rows go by, it occurred to me that this wouldn't be the worst place in the world to hang my hat for a little while. I would have to keep a low profile so that the ranchers that owned the property wouldn't notice me. But since I didn't have much, aside from a blanket, a small transistor radio, and a few other things, I wouldn't leave much of a footprint. And then there were the oranges. An abundance of food, for a starving body and soul.

"I need to give it a tune-up. It should run much smoother after I finish with it!" Jules shouted, his voice pulling me away from my thoughts.

"Yeah. I like this truck," I responded disinterestedly.

When we got back to my mother's apartment, I stepped from the truck and leaned back into the open window, "Let's catch up soon" I said.

"Yeah, stop by. I may be able to land us a job with a real estate guy. His name is Zuckerman, he is a friend of my mom's. He needs some ditches dug," he yelled back.

"I'd be interested. Let me know," I shouted as he pulled away.

My mother was sitting in the living room watching television when I walked into the apartment. She looked exhausted. "That was Jules. He just bought that truck and is fixing it up," I said.

"There is some food on the kitchen counter if you want some," she replied. I thanked her and walked into the kitchen. "Kevin, I'm going to have to ask you to leave the apartment. You know I don't want you to go, but social services will be visiting any day now and I just can't risk you staying here right now. It could jeopardize my welfare status. Do you understand?"

"I understand. You have given me two days already. I'll be gone in a few minutes." Crushed, I gathered the few things that I had and stepped outside.

"Please stop by and visit soon," she said. "Welcome back Kevin."

There was an old railroad bed that ran behind my mother's apartment. The tracks had once transported citrus out of the valley until trucking rose in popularity and rendered the tracks obsolete. They had since been torn up but the trackbed remained. It followed a narrow strip of land and ended at a packing plant located on the east end of Ojai. I hit the old bed and started walking.

An hour later, I arrived back at the orchard on Grand Avenue. I scaled one of the stone walls and stood atop it to assess the situation. There were no houses close by. I was at the far end of the property boundary of one orchard, a location where my chance of being detected was low. I looked around for a decent spot to sleep. The trees had shallow irrigation ditches at their bases but I could make a relatively even surface by moving a small amount of soil to create a level surface. A small utility tractor sputtered in the distance, but far enough away that I did not worry. I hopped down off of the wall and sat peacefully for a few hours at the base of a tree. As the sun began to set, the orange glow on the rows of trees reminded me of a George Inness landscape I'd seen in one of my mother's art books. The hue was soft and luminescent. Crickets sang their sweet melody and with my back against the trunk of a tree, I drifted off to sleep. Little did I know, this orchard would be my home for months to come.

17.

THE NEXT DAY, I woke up from a restless sleep. Fog laid like a thick blanket over the orchard. I had shifted my body position continuously all night trying to get comfortable, and my back felt stiff from the uneven ground. The only noise I heard was the periodic sound of cars passing on the nearest rural road. Luckily, the stone wall kept me hidden from passersby on the road. The trees above me were speckled with ripe oranges, begging to be picked. As I reached up to pluck one of the low-hanging fruits for breakfast, I quickly scanned the area for people. Trespassing and stealing made me uneasy, but I didn't have any other options. Necessity outweighed my hesitancy to break the law. It had been less than forty-eight hours since leaving the house on Evergreen Drive, yet the time which had passed seemed like weeks. I had no plan, no agenda. The only thing I had going was to wait to hear from Jules about the possibility of part-time work.

As I peeled an orange, the amazing fragrance that it produced overwhelmed me. It had been so long since I'd had fresh fruit, that I experienced a newfound appreciation for it. The extreme joy that I felt at that moment eclipsed all of my concerns. I had a new perspective on life. The importance that I placed on common things such as fruit, had been altered to such a degree over the past five months, that basic human necessities were all that really mattered to me. I yearned only for love, shelter, and nourishment, things that most people take for granted each and every day. As I consumed the orange, it tasted remarkably sweet. I relished every bite and smiled as its juice ran down my chin. Four oranges later, I rolled the radio and a few other items up in my blanket and tucked them at the base of the tree trunk. I then climbed the rock wall, looking around for people as I did, and started down Grand Avenue. The morning fog had begun to lift and cars now filtered up and down the road. I elected not to hitchhike, but to take in the sights and smells of Ojai. I wanted to fill my senses with home.

An hour later, I arrived at the front door of Jules' house. His truck was parked out on the street so I assumed that he was home. I knocked a few times, but no one answered, so I sat down on the curb and patiently waited. The sky overhead was now clear and the heat of the sun had substantially increased. It was another hot day. A few minutes later, Jules greeted me from his open bedroom window, "Hey, I'm just waking up. I'll be out in about ten minutes."

I looked around the street and recalled how I used to pass by these same houses on my way home from a nearby park. Being back in Ojai flooded my mind with memories of my youth. It seemed like such a long time ago.

"Thanks for waiting," Jules said as he came out of the house.

"Any word on that job?' I asked.

"Yeah, let's go up there now," he said as he walked towards his truck.

Fifteen minutes later, we reached a small open area off of the side of Cuyama Road. In it, there was another very narrow, unevenly paved road that meandered through a dry field dotted with oak trees. We drove slowly, the truck bounced from divots and potholes in the worn pavement. The eroded road ended at two small buildings, one of which was an open storage structure. There were shovels and a pulaski laid out as if waiting for us. I walked around the building. It was open on one side with a small room at the far north end. The room was empty and the floor was covered with sawdust. There was one window that allowed enough sunlight to filter across the sawdust floor and I was instantly reminded of an Andrew Wyeth painting from a book that my grandfather possessed.

"Do you think the owner would let me stay in this room for a while?" I asked Jules.

"Wow, this is kinda cool. I don't know. Let's ask him. Let me show you the job first. He wants us to dig a ditch through the road right here and put a drainage pipe in," Jules said as he pointed to the ground. I reached for the pulaski and immediately started pummeling the asphalt. The temperature had already reached 98 °F. Sweat poured from my forehead as I relegated all of my strength to the job at hand, determined to penetrate the thickness of the asphalt.

"This is going to take a while!" I yelled. As I paused for air, a Mercedes Benz pulled up to where Jules and I worked, and a large man lifted himself from the driver's seat. His ruddy face was covered with beads of sweat and his collared shirt indicated that he was a professional man.

"Hello, boys. I see you are already at it. Good job. I'll pay you four dollars an hour. I'm Mr. Zuckermann," he said as he walked toward me, extending his arm to shake hands.

"I'm Kevin," I replied.

"Jules tells me you are a good worker. You two are going to need every bit of strength to get through this ugly stuff," he laughed as he spoke. "I'll let you guys get back to work. Let me know if there is anything you need."

When he pulled away, we resumed digging. About two hours later, I stopped to assess our progress and realized that this was a much more strenuous task than I had originally thought. Jules appeared to be suffering from heat exhaustion and went to lay down in the shade. I continued to dig. If Mr. Zuckermann was pleased with our work, I thought, then he might be amicable to allow me to stay in his storage shed for a while.

At four-thirty in the afternoon, the ditch was finally completed. We laid a small ABS pipe in place and then buried it with a bag of prepared asphalt that Mt. Zuckermann had left for the job.

Just as we were finishing, a cloud of dust rolled in behind the Mercedes.

"You kids done?" he yelled from his open window.

"Yeah, we're just filling it in now," said Jules. "Mr. Zuckermann, are you using that little room for anything? Kevin and I think it's cool and we would like to crash there for a while if that would be okay with you?"

"Well, I don't see why not, at least for a few weeks. Just don't mess things up and leave it like you found it and it should be fine," he replied.

"Thank you, we'll make sure we clean it up even before we crash in it," I said.

"You guys have been out here for about five hours. I owe you twenty-five dollars apiece. Does that sound good?" he asked as he opened the car door. We both agreed.

He walked over and handed each of us money. As I held it in my hand, my mind raced with the possibility of sitting in a restaurant for a real meal. As Mr. Zuckermann pulled away, the heat and dryness of the parched landscape was punctuated by the dust thrown in the air behind the Mercedes. Jules and I placed the tools back where we'd found them and returned to the little room. Without much ventilation, it was stale and hot inside. Though the afternoon temperature had dropped to 90°F, we quickly stepped back outside.

"What time is it?" I asked.

"6 o'clock," Jules said. "There is a good Mexican restaurant in town. They have a special burrito that's huge! Do you want to go check it out?" he asked.

"Yeah, let's go!" I exclaimed excitedly.

When we pulled into the restaurant parking lot, it was already crowded with cars and motorcycles. A short line had formed at the entrance so we stepped in and waited patiently, admiring a small group of chopped motorbikes parked next to the waiting line. They were all very well taken care of, their chrome so polished that they sparkled and shimmered like water. I remembered from rumors to keep a distance from any motorcycle that may belong to a member of a gang. These bikes probably did, so we exercised caution as we looked at the machines with delight, all the while making sure to keep our distance.

"You guys like those, huh?" asked a deep-throated voice from behind. I turned to see three men walking toward us. Two were dressed in Levi jeans and jackets, the other in leather chaps. I was struck by the physical enormity of the two men in jeans. The third was relatively thin and much older than the others.

"Where are you guys from?" Jules asked.

"Oxnard. We come up here to exercise these bikes a little. You guys live around here?" asked the oldest of the three.

"Yeah," replied Jules casually. Then, the men walked away from their bikes and to the side of the restaurant, one of the men gestured for us to follow.

"Do you know a lot of people in Ojai?" asked the oldest.

"Yeah, we know enough I guess. Why?" Jules said. I chose to remain silent. I was somewhat intimidated by their presence.

"Well, I'll tell you what. We need some help here. We have several business transactions going on and need help selling up here. There's good money in it," he said.

"What is it you guys want us to do?" Jules asked.

"Move some opium for us. It's easy. You keep quiet about the whole thing and it will be a lot easier than digging ditches," he said laughing. I was shocked. How had he known the work that we had just completed without us mentioning it? The older man continued.

"We give you the stash and you move it. We'll collect every week. You guys rat and you'll wind up somewhere where no one will ever find ya. Just play it straight, do what we ask and you can keep some personal stash for yourself. Sound good?" He looked at the other two men with a grin. Jules and I both looked at each other and shook our heads without pausing.

"Okay, we'll do it."

"Meet us here Monday night. We'll have two separate –" The older man stopped mid-sentence and glared at a few people who were looking at their bikes. The onlookers made a few comments to each other and then moved on. He continued talking, "We'll have a stash for you guys and we'll tell you what we want out of it. You tell them this is pure smack and it ain't cut with anything. If you get taken, you are responsible. We'll give you a week to move the shit and then come collect in a week. Do you understand?"

"Yes," I replied slowly.

"No rats. Am I clear?" exclaimed one of the bigger men as he glared down at the two of us. The three men then moved slowly back to their bikes, the oldest turned to us with a smirk and gave us a thumbs up. Jules and I stood stunned in the shadows of the side of the restaurant as the men started their motorcycles. The roar was so loud it drowned out the traffic noise from the passing cars.

Jules and I sat in one of the restaurant booths furthest from the entrance and discussed with hushed voices the recent deal as we ate our meal. The restaurant was full of patrons that night, some of which looked familiar. I felt nervous, as I'm sure Jules did, though we did not share this apprehension with one another. Perhaps this was in an effort to instill confidence between us.

"Hey, why don't we go get your stuff and we'll go back to Zuckermann's shed tonight?" asked Jules.

"That sounds great," I responded.

Once we got back to the orchard, I had a difficult time locating where I had slept the night before. The tree canopy shut out any ambient light and the sheer darkness intensified as I went from tree to tree. Jules kept his truck idling while I searched from one row of citrus to the next. After about ten minutes, I located the blanket with my things wrapped inside. I climbed over the stone wall, threw everything in the back of the truck, and jumped inside. We drove over to Jules' house and while he went inside to collect his things, I remained in the truck. Twenty minutes passed, during which I thought about our new job. As I sat there waiting, I began to think that Jules had either gotten side-tracked or there was a problem. It shouldn't take him this long to collect the few things for bedding. So, I got out of the pickup and walked up to the house. Just as I got to the door, Jules emerged empty-handed. He appeared agitated. "What's up?" I asked.

"My mom doesn't want me staying up there. She's not in a good mood," he explained with frustration. "I didn't mow the backyard like I was supposed to, now I'm grounded I guess."

"I'll take you up there. I'm allowed to do that at least," he said as he climbed back into the truck. When we pulled away from the curb, he asked, "Have you ever smoked opium?"

"No. What's it like?" I questioned, leaning towards him so he could hear me over the truck's loud rumbling.

"I've never tried it. But it looks like we are going to see what kinda high we get from it. I hear it's good!" he shouted back.

When we got back to Mr. Zuckermann's shed, there was an eerie absence of light. The only noise was the hauntingly beautiful sound of cricket song in the dry fields. The night temperature had cooled a bit but was still in the eighties. Jules was anxious to get back home, as he did not want to further aggravate his already angered mother. I waved to him as he backed up and pulled the truck into a tight turnaround. It churned up clouds of dust as it moved down the decayed drive.

Silence was all that was left when I walked into the little room. The smell of sawdust permeated the dark interior. I laid down my wool blanket and went through the few articles I'd brought with me from Oregon. There was a paperback book about the Wright Brothers, a few pairs of socks, underwear, and the small pipe which used to sit on the window sill on Evergreen Drive. I sat with my back supported by the wall and thought about the journey that pipe had gone on, from the bench in Ventura, to the house on Evergreen, and now, back to Ojai. I again wondered where that old man was now, and whether or not I'd ever run into him again? Still sitting and holding the pipe, I drifted off to sleep.

I awoke to the noise of a car engine shutting off just outside of the little room where I was sleeping. Then silence persisted for what seemed like an hour. I don't know exactly because I drifted back to sleep. Perhaps I had dreamt of the car, I could not be sure. When I finally came to, my arms were sore from the previous day's digging. My back was stiff and my whole body ached. I rolled onto my side in an attempt to find relief. I was cold, uneasy and my constant movements would not provide relief. I tried to fall back to sleep but to no avail. Suddenly, a hand grabbed a hold of my arm. My heart lurched and my body stiffened in shock. I was afraid and speechless. The grasp was strong and felt tremendously painful on my sore muscles. I instinctively rolled to the side to free my other arm but as I did so, another hand grabbed ahold of me. I was lying face down so I could not see what was happening, what felt like a forearm pressed firmly against the back of my neck. The weight of it was like an enormous block of cement. I was trapped, immobile, defenseless. My heart raced and I began to hyperventilate, gasping through the dusty air. Things happened so quickly that I had no time to think, only to rely on involuntary reactions. I could smell alcohol emanating from a man's breath as he bent my arm backward, keeping me motionless. His left hand grabbed for the waist of my pants, and I squirmed rabidly to get away, my entire body seized. Finally, he managed to get a grip on my waistband and forcefully pulled my pants down, scratching the side of my leg as he tore off my bottoms. My breath had become more labored, dust-filled my lungs as the full weight of the man pressed upon me. I had no ability to cry or yell. I felt like I was suffocating, was I about to die? Is this all of the life I got? Consciousness left me. I faded away, my body and mind unable to endure the trauma.

When I came to and opened my eyes, darkness shrouded me. I had lost all reference, I did not know where I was or what had happened. Had I just had a horrific dream? As I tried to turn my head, I experienced extreme pain in my neck. My back felt like I'd been struck by a bat. The phlegm in my throat was thick with dust. It was a challenge for me to breathe. My shirt was drenched. I was so wet I thought someone must have poured water on me. What had happened? My pants were down around my ankles, my underwear was gone. Where was I? It was too dark to get my bearings. I tried to stand but immediately collapsed, my scrawny legs were too weak to support my underweight physique. I felt an excruciating pain in my rectum and testicles which grew in intensity as I tried to move. I was immobile. I could not walk, I felt paralyzed from the waist down. I laid on my back in an effort to alleviate the pain, but to no avail. Minutes passed like hours, the hours passed like days.

As the early morning light trickled in through the window, my surroundings began to materialize like they were forming through a dark background. My underwear was laying on the ground about five feet from where I lay. My wool blanket was bundled in one corner of the room with my other belongings close by. My body was covered in sawdust and I continuously coughed up thick phlegm. Exhaustion overcame me and I dropped back into sleep.

My eyes flickered open to a room bathed in heat and sunlight. It was already afternoon. The entire morning had vanished, gone forever. It wasn't until about five o'clock in the afternoon that I was finally able to peel myself from the ground and collect my few belongings. I had to get out of there. I wanted to remove this place from my memory, forever. Movement was difficult, slow, and painful. I walked gingerly down the uneven drive, until I came to a large oak tree located at the bottom of the hill, and stopped to rest. I stayed put for approximately fifteen minutes, then a light blue sedan pulled up and the woman driving stopped to ask if I needed help. She looked familiar, perhaps she was the mother of a classmate in junior high? Her voice was soft and kind.

"You look like a mess. Do you need a ride?" she asked through the car window. I cleared my throat a few times.

"Yes, please," was all I could get out. I tried to form words but they only hurt my throat. I opened the passenger door and climbed in. "Where are you heading?" I asked softly.

"I'm on my way home. I live on Shady Lane. Are you sure you're okay?" she inquired. I nodded.

To this day, I don't know why I didn't reveal to her what had happened. I don't think I'd had a chance to process the previous day's events. Nor do I think I'd had the time to let the shock wear off. I felt so much shame, perhaps I had deserved this. Once again, I felt insignificant. I was no different than the trash blowing around on the ground at the Ventura bus station.

"Can you drop me off on the corner of your street?" I asked. She did not reply but kept driving. Her demeanor was calm and kind. On her left hand, she wore a ring. I attempted to scratch out some words.

"Do you have any kids?" I asked, coughing through my question.

"Yes. I have three girls, two are now young adults," she said proudly.

I held back tears as I imagined her devotion to her husband and children. As I watched the town of Ojai pass by bathed by the intense summer sun, I thought of my brothers and their situation of starvation and abuse. This woman's presence strengthened my desire to be back with my brothers, the only family I really had. As we stopped at the corner of her street, daylight had begun to fade.

"Thank you for the lift," I said as I slowly rose from the car seat. She smiled and continued to drive on.

I did not want to see Jules at that time. I needed to be alone. I headed up the road in the direction of the orchard. The pain in my groin region intensified with every step. The strength in my legs was spent and I had to take periodic rests along the way.

I finally reached the orchard at about nine o'clock in the evening, and I stopped and stood, staring at the looming stone wall. How was I to get over it? I summoned every amount of strength I had left in my puny, famished body. Eventually, I made it over, but it was not an easy task. It had required a herculean effort that night. After falling to the ground on the orchard side of the wall, I peeled myself up and walked a few steps between the trees. I plucked a few oranges to satisfy my hunger and placed my sparse belongings at the base of the tree I chose to sleep under that night. I then squatted very gingerly to sit in the soft dirt. Crickets sang their soothing lullaby to me while I ate, it was the only true and beautiful thing in that moment. Their song was all that gave me hope and took me away from the pain I was experiencing in that moment.

18.

THE NEXT MORNING, fog once again shrouded the valley. It was six-thirty a.m. and the streets were still quiet. I lay on my side under the wool blanket. It still smelled faintly of my old friend, the goat. I recollected about how this blanket, the one I now laid under, had once provided warmth for that sweet goat during the last few days of its life. I then shuddered at the thought of its untimely demise. It had been preventable. I now found myself in a strikingly similar situation.

My back ached, soreness lingered in the fresh aftermath of the trauma I had just endured. But I was able to move my neck without as much pain. My legs were also working better after a citrus dinner and another night of sleep, standing was easier. I got up and moved ever so slowly to a makeshift hole I'd dug before to use as a temporary toilet. The pain was still present but I welcomed the return of strength in my legs. What was usually a mundane task of relieving myself, turned into a torturous event. I felt as if knives were being stabbed into my rectum. Once finished, I looked down into the hole, the bottom of which was now covered with fresh blood. I returned to my solitary blanket and laid back down. Sleep immediately overtook me.

When I opened my eyes again, the fog had evaporated and the sun was directly overhead. Faint voices could be heard from the ranch house in the distance. About one hundred yards away, I noticed two men walking in my direction. They appeared to be carefully inspecting the trees as they walked. I froze, careful not to move. Surely my presence would soon be discovered. Should I run, I thought? Or stay and try to explain my situation? Either way, I knew I would have to reconcile with the owners of the ranch. One of the two men saw me but continued on, looking over the trees as he walked. He seemed un-interested, which surprised me. They continued in my direction. As they approached one of them spoke to me.

"How are you today? No need to be alarmed, son. I've been aware of you since you first got here. We ranchers tend to know what is happening in our orchards."

"I just needed a place to sleep, sir. I will leave," I said in an apologizing tone.

"Kinda young, aren't you? What did you do, run away from home or something?" he asked with a smile.

"No sir. My parents are in a situation where they can't take care of me," I replied.

"Well, I'll tell you what. As long as you don't vandalize the property or throw oranges at cars, you can continue to stay," he said as he continued his inspection.

"Do you need any help with work?" I asked.

"Not at this time, but if something comes up, I'll let you know," he said as he turned to the next row and disappeared behind the trees.

I sat back down, completely drained of energy from standing for the duration of the brief conversation. Again, I realized that I was drenched in sweat. Perhaps this time it was from the heat, or the fear of being found out, or both. I felt like I had been drugged with a sedative. I found even the slightest movements to be difficult, and I could not stay awake. After my encounter with the ranchers, I fell back to sleep almost immediately.

The next time I opened my eyes, I was surrounded in darkness. Stars twinkled in the sky above. Once again, I'd lost track of time. But, that did not matter as I had nowhere to go. I struggled to find a position to lessen the pain. Finally, after a few hours, I found that laying on my right side relieved much of my discomfort. The ambient sound of crickets proved to be my only comfort, but it was the best medicine I could have asked for. Each night their songs carried me off to sleep, just like when I was a child and my grandfather used to read bedtime stories to me.

On Monday morning, I awoke to dampness on my wool blanket and on the soil where I lay. The pain in my back had lessened and I felt my mobility had improved as I got up to move around. The morning fog had already lifted, a small covey of quail were gathered a few rows away from me and were pecking at the ground in search of food. As they moved in unison, I felt a sense of contentment well up within me. It was a welcome feeling.

"Hey, Kevin. Are you up yet?" a voice called from over the wall. Jules was clamoring over the stone wall. "I went up to the room at Zuckerman's place and didn't see you or your things there, so I guessed you had come back here. Didn't you like it up there?" he asked.

I did the best I could to disguise my pain as I slowly rose from my spot under the tree. He was wearing blue jeans and a short-sleeved orange shirt and walked toward me with an energetic gait. He continued, "Mr. Zuckerman said there is more work to do at the ranch house and wondered if you still were interested in staying up there?"

I planned to keep secret what happened and had no intention of telling Jules about my ordeal. I was terribly ashamed and I knew that I must not let anyone find out. My self-esteem had already been crushed. If my own parents could not love me before, how could anyone love me now? I had been let down so many times by people, I knew that I would get no real support from anyone. I'd learned to solely rely on myself, that was my only safety net. I had matured overnight, from a young teen to a grown adult. And I knew that if I did not become mentally tough, I would not survive this world for very long.

"Nah. I don't feel like working up there anymore. We're still meeting with those guys tonight, right?" I said, changing the subject.

"Yeah. Let's do it," Jules replied. We sat for a while and Jules told me about the new stereo he had just purchased. He then invited me over to listen to the various albums he had accumulated. Movement was definitely easier for me now, my legs had regained most of their strength. I tucked my blanket under the citrus tree and we climbed the wall. I found it quite a lot easier than the previous night.

"Do you want something to eat?" he asked as we pulled into his driveway.

"That would be great! Do you think your mother will mind?" I asked with concern.

"Don't worry, she and my aunt went to Ventura to do some shopping, come on in." I devoured the bowl of cold cereal Jules placed in front of me. He put a Black Sabbath album on the turntable and cranked the volume. The music was so loud it could have deafened the noise of a jet engine.

"Listen to the clarity!" he screamed above the noise. "Do you still want to meet up with those guys tonight!?" I nodded. My shouting couldn't outdo that of Ozzy Osborne's. Jules got the message and turned the volume down a bit.

"Hey, if you want to throw your clothes in the washing machine, go ahead. They look dirtier than me!" Jules teased.

"Heck yeah," I replied as I stripped down. I removed a few items from my pocket, including the small pipe. We sat and discussed our elaborate plans for the future. Jules would own a mechanic shop that would build custom dragsters and I would be a plastic surgeon. We would visit each other's mansions on occasion, and he would have a foxy wife. I would build an estate on the beach where I could surf anytime I liked.

I rose to use the bathroom, and instantly worried, would there be blood this morning? The pain was still present but it was not as severe. I glanced into the toilet afterward, there was only a little blood. I was recovering.

I walked back into the living room. The curtains were closed but the brightness of the sun illuminated them in such a way that they looked like they were on fire. The heat from outside bled through the windows. It was so warm in the house that Jules suggested we take a drive down to the beach to cool off. We waited for my clothes to finish drying and then we headed for the truck.

"You never told me much about Oregon. What happened when you were there?" he asked as we drove.

"It was rough and I think it's only gonna get worse for my brothers. I wish I could help them. I'm just glad to be back. I can't really live with my mom so I'll keep looking for a place to stay," I said.

"How come you don't want to stay in Zuckerman's shed?" he shouted over the noise of the pickup.

"I just didn't feel comfortable up there. I like the orchard better," I said as I looked away. I hoped he would not inquire any further. I changed the subject again and asked him about his truck. Jules liked to talk about that old Ford pickup so I knew I'd be safe steering the conversation in that direction.

As we got closer to the ocean, the oppressive heat in the air was replaced by a cool coastal breeze. There was a bank of fog hovering above the beach. It demarcated the inland area from the coast. The cloud-covered shoreline was peppered with seagulls. The scene of serenity bathed my senses and cooled me both physically and emotionally. The day at the beach was a blur, time flew as we basked in the salt air and cool temperatures which nourished our bodies.

Before I knew it, it was five o'clock and we were headed back to Ojai. We passed by heat-scorched fields that reminded me of summers long past. Then Jules turned off of the freeway and onto Creek Road, a rural drive that paralleled a creek, and we wound through sycamore trees and past quaint homes. The road came out near the Mexican restaurant where we'd agreed to meet the bikers the previous Friday.

The parking lot was empty when we arrived. Jules killed the engine and we waited.

"I want to join the Navy as soon as I turn seventeen," he said.

"Really? Are you not happy at home?" I asked.

"My mom and I really don't get along. She has said to me numerous times that she wants me out of the house when I turn eighteen. I also think it would be great to see other parts of the world. I guess I'm getting tired of Ojai. What I want to do is –"

He stopped short when we heard the roar of Harley-Davidsons pull into the parking lot. We flung open the truck doors in unison and hopped out. We wanted to show them our presence, and for them to know we'd come alone to the rendezvous point. There were only two men this time. The older of the two dismounted his motorcycle and gestured for us to follow him behind the building. The other stayed on his bike and stood guard. The older biker looked from side to side, scanning the parking lot. Then, he reached into the inside pocket of his leather jacket and pulled out a paper bag. It was wrapped around something the shape of a small cylinder. Slowly, he unfurled the bag and pulled out a can of Pepsi.

"There are thirty grams of pure smack in here boys, each bundled. This is white powder heroin, not that brown powder shit. You tell your marks this is eighty-six percent pure, high-grade stuff and it ain't cut with nothing. We want twenty-five a gram. You can keep a gram for yourself. Meet us back here Friday at the same time. Now I can trust you guys, right? Don't even think about fucking with me because I'll track your sorry asses down, you understand? You do this right and I'll take care of you. No ratting, you got it?" he said as he wrapped the can back up and handed it to me. Jules and I nodded in unison.

"Don't fuck with me!" he yelled over his shoulder as he walked back to his bike. The two men kick-started their choppers and roared out of the parking lot. Neither one looked back as they rode away. Jules and I walked back to the truck in silence. I realized that I was holding onto the can exceedingly tight, white-knuckled, for dear life.

"Do you know who'd even want this stuff?" I asked him.

"Yeah. My neighbor said she would buy all of it. We already have it all sold," he said with a big smile.

"Do you wanna try some from our cut?" I asked.

"Yeah. Let's go back down to Creek Road."

Night had fallen by the time we made it to a small pullout off of Creek Road. It was pitch black out. Light from the moon was screened by the thick grove of trees. But the night wasn't eerie, it was peaceful. Frogs croaked and the creek ran gently over river rocks below the road.

"Damn. We don't have anything to smoke this with. Let me see if there is an empty can or something behind the seat," Jules said.

"Hold on. I've got the perfect thing!" I exclaimed. I reached into my pants pocket and pulled out the small yellow pipe.

"Where did you get that?" he asked. I gave him the brief background story of the pipe, and told him that it had been my one companion on my foray to Oregon and back. It was the only thing of mine that Lynn had not discarded the day she went through our things.

I turned the Pepsi can upside down and gave it a small shake. Out came two bundles. I kept one and dropped the other back into the empty container. As I carefully opened the small, folded brown paper, I found what looked like baking powder. Never having seen heroin before, I was amazed at its luminescent quality, it almost glowed.

"Pack it in the pipe and let's light 'er up!" Jules said anxiously.

I placed a very small amount in the pipe's bowl, not knowing the amount typically used. When I finished packing the smack, Jules struck a match, illuminating the cab of the old Ford. I brought the pipe to my mouth, the flame to the powder, and slowly inhaled. Immediately, I started to cough, my lungs were not used to any kind of smoke. It tasted harsh, yet pungent at the same time. The smoke smelled similar to burning hair, but with a milder odor. It was almost fragrant.

I passed the pipe to Jules and watched with intent. As he inhaled, the contents of the bowl glowed softly. He grasped the steering wheel firmly as he tried to contain the smoke in his lungs. Then he exhaled and handed the pipe back to me. I lifted the pipe back to my lips and inhaled again, this time I managed to hold the smoke in without coughing. I then handed the pipe back to Jules and my arm seemed to lengthen, as if it were stretching to reach him. My movements had slowed down but remained deliberate. The cab of the truck began to expand. I could not tell if it was enlarging or if I was shrinking. The atmosphere became still and deeply silent. Jules moved his feet on the truck floor and the sound echoed as if we were in a tunnel. The croaking of frogs became noticeable now and filled the cab like a thick pea soup. Their song became louder and louder with each passing minute. It was somewhat soothing, and I thought they were talking to me in a language I had yet to translate but somehow understood. Each time I attempted to raise my arms or turn my head, the movement felt uncontrollably slow, as if I was encased in cement. I felt like the weight of my gaunt body might crush the seat I was sitting on. I looked at Jules, his lips moved but no sound came out. I continued to stare fixedly at him. His head grew into an amphora, an ancient Egyptian clay pot used for carrying water. His lips looked like two salamanders moving in unison. I was enthralled by his appearance. I then discovered that my body was free from pain for the first time in days. Though my head felt like it weighed as much as the truck that we were sitting in. I did not have the strength to hold it up any longer so I leaned over and rested it on the truck bench. The frogs continued to talk to me. They guided me on my journey to an undisclosed destination. I felt surprisingly comfortable. I no longer had a worry in the world.

The next thing I remember was waking up on the ground amidst fallen oak leaves. Morning light filtered down through the tree limbs above. I rose slowly, trying to get my bearings. I had been lying about thirty feet from the truck. Everything was still, there was no frog song. The only thing I heard was the creek rushing over rocks. My back was sore and my throat was parched. My entire body hurt. I felt exhausted, like I'd just run an ultramarathon.

I shouted towards the truck, "Jules! Jules!"

A faint voice replied from the cab, "I'm here, goddamnit. I think I pissed my pants."

I stood up slowly but found it difficult to regain my balance as I walked over to the truck. With each step, my coordination improved.

"Are you okay?" I asked as I neared the open window.

"Yeah. Man, I feel like I got run over by a train," he said softly.

"How did I end up way over there?" I asked Jules.

"You kept saying that the frogs wanted you to visit them. I tried to stop you because I wasn't sure where you were going," Jules coughed as he replied. We both started to laugh uncontrollably. Neither one of us could pull it together. It took a good ten minutes to finally regain my composure. I sat down on the ground with my back against the front truck tire. The wind began to gently blow and rustle the leaves on the ground where I had spent the night. They performed a beautifully choreographed dance specifically for me. I watched in amazement.

"We should go. My mom is going to start worrying if she isn't already," said Jules.

I dragged myself from the ground and loaded into the pickup. Jules turned the key but the engine would not start. A few expletives left Jules' hoarse throat. He tried again. This time, the engine came to life and dumped a cloud of exhaust behind the truck. I grabbed the pipe off of the dashboard of the truck and held it tightly in my left hand. It felt more substantial than it had the night before and its surface looked more elegant than I had remembered. Little did I know, that small pipe was to become my best ally, the only friend that would not desert me.

19.

ONE WEEK HAD passed since my inaugural taste of opium, and I had indulged in it every evening since. I hadn't seen Jules much since the night on Creek Road. The powder called to me daily, it had become my only friend. I finally had the relationship that I'd sought after for so long.

One morning in the orchard, as sunlight streamed through the treetops, I sat gazing at the empty paper bindle cast aside on the dirt beside me. The heroin was gone. It had been my only companion, my sole compatriot, the only friend that could help me to escape my pain.

The fog had lifted and the fragrance of orange blossoms swept through the orchard grove like a fine mist. The covey of quail had returned, their heads bobbed as they moved from one row of trees to the next. I sat there for hours, contemplating my surroundings. Green leaves speckled by bright orange dashes of color stood out in contrast to the dark brown of the rich soil. I felt like I was sitting in a freshly finished Pissaro painting. I was perfectly calm and present, it was an enlightening experience.

A shout from behind suddenly broke my trance. "Hey young man!" I looked over my shoulder and saw one of the ranchers approaching. "Are you still interested in work?" he asked. "My co-worker owns some property on the east end and he has an irrigation dam that needs to be painted. Are you interested?"

"Yeah. When would he want me to start?" I asked.

"He's coming around in about an hour. I'll have him come over and you two fellas can meet," he said as he walked past me, en route to examine irrigation lines.

While I waited, I climbed atop the stone wall and started walking. I recalled the history of these walls which was well known throughout the valley. They had been constructed by Chinese laborers at the turn of the century. And over the years, folks had on occasion found empty opium bottles tucked in between the stones, that had once been placed there by the workers. I thought of the irony.

A warm breeze came from the east and moved through the leaves, making a rustling noise. The covey of quail were now moving in harmonious, rhythmic motions along the rows of trees. The air was clear and crisp that morning. After an hour, I returned to the base of the tree where I'd chosen to rest my weary body. There was no one in sight so I sat and waited. Another twenty minutes passed before I noticed a short man in coveralls striding towards me from the direction of the ranch house. He said nothing until he was within a few feet of where I sat. "Gene tells me you may be interested in some work?" he asked. I stood to reply to his question.

"Yes sir. He said something about a dam that needs painting?"

"It's up at the top of Dennison Grade. I can take you up there and show you what needs to be done. Is now a good time?" he questioned.

"Yes, now is good," I said.

As he turned and walked back toward the ranch house, I noticed that he walked with a slight limp. I got up and followed him. I had not yet seen the ranch owner's house. Its whitewashed walls looked as if they were freshly painted and the red shingled roof blazed like fire under the summer sun. A clothesline at the side of the house supported several pairs of work shirts and faded pants, as a breeze tried to dissuade them from their clothespins. A large pepper tree framed the front of the home. I was struck with the memory of the grand giant that had once stood sentry at my childhood home. Bright red peppercorns were strewn across the lawn and gravel driveway of the ranch house. The deep, cool shade cast by the large tree was inviting. A solitary old red pickup truck was parked in front of the stone walk that led to the front door.

"By the way, I'm Bob. Climb on in," he said as he opened the driver's door of the red pickup. We drove down the long drive and up the winding grade that led to the worksite. During the ride, I gave him a brief summary of my story and why I was squatting in the orchard. I mentioned how I was appreciative that the owner of the orchard generously allowed me to stay for the time being.

"Yes sir. Gene is a good old boy and I'm sure he doesn't

mind at all, as long as you don't abuse things," he said with a smile.

It was about noon and the temperature was over one hundred degrees when we pulled off onto a dirt road that ran through a field dotted with large oak trees. Rolling waves of amber grasses extended from the base of the sage-covered Topa Topa mountains beyond the large field. We briefly stopped in the shade of a gracious large oak and then continued on to a narrow ravine.

Bob pointed down to a small rusted dam constructed of steel below us.

"The first thing we need to do is sandblast all of that rust off. Then we'll paint 'er with

a primer and finish coat. You up for it son?" he asked, wiping the sweat from his forehead.

"Yes. I think I can do that," I said.

"I'll give you a hundred bucks for the whole job. I'll have the sandblaster and ladder here for you tomorrow if you want to start then," he hollered as he turned to head for the shade.

I followed him, my shoes sank deep into the dirt road, and dust rose with every step. The smell of the weeds and dry grass was strong. The shade of the oak tree under which the truck was parked was a welcome departure from the heat, even for a brief reprieve. We loaded back into the pickup and weaved our way down the winding grade to the orchard. It was about two o'clock in the afternoon when we pulled back into the ranch house drive and parked under the large pepper tree.

Things were silent at the house, it appeared to be vacant. The only sound was the breeze whispering through the branches of the great big pepper tree.

"I'll have the sandblaster and the other equipment you'll need up there by tomorrow morning," Bob said as he dropped me off and backed out of the drive.

A cloud of dust obscured the vehicle as it made its way down the road. Once it and the noise of its engine disappeared behind the citrus trees, I was left alone in the solitude of the ranch house. I stood mesmerized for at least ten minutes by the setting of the bright structure nestled amongst the resplendent orange trees. The clothes had since been removed from the line they'd hung from only hours ago. A small rusted harrow and Fresno scraper sat still at one corner of the
driveway and the sunlight reflecting off of the clapboard walls of the house highlighted every bolt and curve of their rusted shapes. I felt that time stood still and that I was in a scene from the American past.

At six o'clock that evening, I sat atop the stone wall that hid my sleeping area from the road and waited for Jules to pick me up for our rendezvous with the bikers. The sun set on the ridge of the purple-colored mountains to the west. Then, I heard the unmistakable noise of Jules' truck before it made its appearance around the curve of the road. The old Ford pickup stopped in a haze of dust and Jules stepped out to lift the hood. "How's it going?" I asked.

"I think my radiator hose is leaking! Hold on a minute!" he shouted over the noise of the truck. After a thorough check, he dropped the hood with a sigh of relief.

"It looks okay," he said. As we loaded into the cab, he continued "My mom has been hassling me. After I sold those twenty-nine g's of smack to the neighbor, I think she suspects something. I'd better not continue selling this stuff or I'm going to get busted. I just know it," Jules said with frustration. "If you want to keep selling though, I'll help find some contacts for you."

"Do you think she'll rat on me?" I asked.

"Nah, you should be good. I'm telling ya though, I gotta get out of the house Kevin! She's being a major bitch," he stated.

As we passed the small buildings that lined the main street of Ojai, my mind conjured ways to find other people to sell to. Not only did I need the money, but I also needed the smack for my growing addiction.

As we neared the restaurant, I strained to locate the motorcycles. The parking lot was nearly empty and the choppers were nowhere to be found. We pulled in and waited. To pass the time, we again discussed our dreams of becoming a mechanic and a medicine man. Red and blue lights from the neon signs in the restaurant's windows illuminated the parking lot's surface as darkness blanketed the valley.

"Do you want to go in and get something to eat?" I asked. Hunger was always on my mind.

"Yeah. How much money do you have? I've got about −"

Jules stopped short, distracted by the deafening roar of motorcycles. Five polished machines slowly pulled into the lot in a single file formation like soldiers lining up for military inspection. Silence fell heavy as they shut their engines down. Jules and I exited the truck and again, the older man signaled for us to follow him behind the restaurant. He glanced around in every direction, scanning for anything suspicious. When he turned to Jules, Jules reached into his pocket and pulled out a wad of cash. He handed it over to the man.

"You guys move it all, huh?" he asked. We nodded in unison. "Good work boys. Did you have any problems?" he asked with a grin as he thumbed through the stack of bills.

"No. We moved it to one person and we took our gram," Jules replied.

The man told us to stay where we were and walked back over to the others who'd remained with the bikes. They talked amongst themselves for about five minutes, then another man dismounted and joined the older one. Together, they walked back into the shadows of the restaurant where we stood.

"We have another fifty grams if you want to move it. We'll give you two g's and fifty bucks for it. Next Monday won't work so make it Friday," the other man said.

"I'm going to drop out. I think my mom is onto me and I don't want to get –" Jules was cut off by the older man.

"You don't know where you got this stuff, you get it? You forget who we are! Do you understand?" he yelled angrily.

"I'll sell it. I can find people to move it to," I said calmly in an effort to reassure him. It was effective and his posture relaxed. I committed to continue selling, more for a source of smack than for the money, money could be earned by other means. I had become addicted to the powder, and it had happened fast. The thought that I would be without the white stuff for even a day felt like an insurmountable challenge. The time I was using was euphoric, but the time that elapsed between the highs moved like molasses. The heroin, surprisingly, served not only as my friend but as a mentor and teacher as well. It gave me insights about life that I was not capable of understanding when I was sober. It guided me beyond my faulty notions and challenged me to learn more about the meaning of my existence.

"We'll see *you* next week," the eldest said as he pointed directly at me.

On the drive back to the orchard, Jules disclosed his neighbor's identity to me. He seemed tense, unusually nervous. "How are you doing?" I asked him.

"I'm really not happy at home. I wanna sell the smack with you and feel I can't because of the old lady. I'm pissed off!" he said, banging his hand on the steering wheel in frustration.

"Come on, let's get high when we get back to the orchard. I'll give you a cut of my stash if you want," I said with my hand on his shoulder. I wanted to reassure him but wasn't sure if my words conveyed it.

"Let's do it," he agreed.

We parked next to the familiar stone wall bordering the orchard and I again thought of the hands that had stacked the wall, stone by stone. According to legend, those same hands had also fallen under the white powder spell. The empty opium bottles wedged between the rocks told the story of their plight, and I found it coincidental that this was the spot I'd chosen to live for the time being.

It was an exceptionally clear night, and stars gleamed against the black background of the heavens. Jules and I sat on the wall with our backs to the orchard. I reached into my pocket for the bag with the bindles. I drew it out and placed it at my side. I took the pipe from my other pocket. It spoke to me without words, taking on a life of its own, comforting me like an old friend. I removed one of the bindles from the bag and carefully unfolded its edges. The white powder glistened like the stars in the night sky.

I meticulously packed the small bowl while Jules expounded on his mechanic shop dreams. His face, painted with delight, was illuminated as he brought a match to the bowl. He too found enchantment in the high. As I adapted to the unique taste, I developed an appetite for the bitter smoke. The more smoke I drew into my lungs, the heavier my body felt. I now believed I must weigh ten tons. I glanced towards Jules, he was lying on his back with his arms over his head as if reaching for something.

I think he was attempting to sing, flat tones left his now enormously large head. I gazed down at my legs, they'd become long strands that extended from my torso all of the way to the road. I tried to move them but was unable to do so. Speaking became an insurmountable task. I tried to utter words but was unsuccessful. A tremendous amount of effort produced only slight movements from my mouth. It was an unbearably arduous task to produce a coherent word. My body found it much easier to join Jules in a prone posture. The pressure on my back from the uneven stones felt good like the wall was massaging the soreness from my chronically stressed musculature. Stars moved in concentric circles and appeared much brighter and more of a yellow hue than before. I grasped the pipe firmly and sensed that it was speaking to me. The concept of God entered my mind and I desired to see him right then and there. I called out mentally, "If you exist, please show yourself. Prove to me that you exist and I'll follow the transcripts of your laws." My focus intensified as I repeated my request over and over again, like a tantric mantra. Jules continued to utter in-comprehensible words, his body was splayed over the old stones like melted taffy in the hot sun. His words drifted into the air with the smoke from the pipe.

It took all of my physical strength to raise my upper body to a sitting position. The weight of my body was extreme, oppressive. Once upright, I looked around and repeated my request to God. My eyes caught a move-ment about one hundred feet from us and to the right, alongside the road. Something was moving towards us, slowly but deliberately. As it neared, it appeared to be a human form. My heart rate increased as the figure walked in our direction. Was this God?

It was cloaked in a long brown raincoat and was of enormous size, perhaps three hundred pounds or more. It had hair that was long and uncombed. When it got closer to us, I realized that it was a woman. Her face appeared confused and angry. A demonstrative crease gouged an indention between her eyebrows. She was wearing some type of rain galoshes and their soles squeaked from the burden of her tremendous weight. She did not so much as glance at us on her way by. I then heard what sounded like an enormous release of flatus, like a wild hog running for a pile of garbage, as it came from her bowels.

I was confused. I'd beckoned God to show himself to me and this is what I saw? I felt demoralized and repulsed by what I'd witnessed. Teachings from my Catholic school, those that mentioned that we were created in the image of God, roared into my psyche like a tsunami hitting a coastal village. Had I gotten a message from the almighty creator? If so, it was traumatic. I hesitated to glance toward the woman, but curiosity got the best of me. I looked down the road in her direction and noticed that she was squatting in the uncut brush at the side of the road, she was urinating. What had happened? Was that really God? I contemplated the experience as I flopped back down on the wall in an uncontrollable manner. Heavy silence lay atop me like a thick blanket, and I fell from consciousness.

20.

I WOKE SLOWLY from my perch on the stone wall. It was still dark and the stones beneath my back were cold. My head was heavy. I looked right and left for Jules, but he was not present. I tried to call out his name but my throat was so parched that I was unable to speak. My entire body felt depleted, and my mind was not able to sift through the thoughts which weaved through its corridors. Sleep arrested me again.

Morning light woke me and I realized that I'd fallen back to sleep. There was no sign of Jules or his truck. I rolled onto my right side in an attempt to alleviate the stomach pain I was experiencing. I laid in that position for an hour, looking down the stone wall adjacent to the road. I wondered how many stones had been gathered to construct this crude, rudimentary structure? Its surface was uneven and the color of the rocks varied from deep green to soft yellow. The sound of the passing vehicles were louder than usual. My hearing was noticeably more sensitive as I reestablished consciousness.

"Hey son, are you feeling okay? I've got the equipment ready for the job up there," Bob shouted as he walked toward me. I rubbed the mat from my eyes and responded.

"Yeah." I felt absolutely depleted, physically and mentally. I gathered myself and climbed down from the wall.

My legs felt disconnected from the rest of my body. I stumbled, which verified the feeling.

"You sure your okay son? You don't look so good," Bob asked with a look of concern.

"I'll be okay. I just stayed up too late last night. Give me a few minutes and I'll meet you at your car," I said. He nodded and turned to walk away. When he'd gone, I quickly, and with much effort, hustled back to the wall in search of the bag of bindles. It sat precariously on the edge of the wall, a large square stone's corner kept it from falling toward the road. I grabbed the bundles and wrapped a brown paper bag firmly around them. I then tucked the package into my wool blanket and hemmed it about the branches of a citrus tree.

My legs regained some of their strength as I jogged awkwardly toward Bob's small truck that sat idling under the large pepper tree. Bob and Gene were engaged in conversation on the front porch of the house when I arrived, so I climbed into the truck cab and waited. After a few minutes, Bob appeared.

"I'll catch up with you later!" he told Gene. "You sure you are feeling up for work today?" he asked me again as we drove. "It's a lot of work. I'll have to show you how to operate the sandblaster," he said. Then he reached down to a small box that sat on the floorboard and pulled out a sandwich. He extended it to me, "Do you want this?"

"Yes, thank you!" I exclaimed as I reached for the sandwich in a hurry, for fear it might escape me.

We arrived at the small rusted dam at nine o'clock in the morning and were greeted by the summer heat and swarms of flies. Two other men were already down in the ravine at the base of the dam. Bob explained that these men worked for him and were setting up the equipment for me to use. He stepped out of the truck and shouted down to them that he needed them to get to another job. I hopped out of the pickup and picked my way down the steep wall of the ravine, sending dirt and small rocks from the bank as I went.

When I got to the bottom, I assessed the metal structure that I was to paint. It was about twenty feet high and thirty feet wide. It was covered in thick rust, its unique design indicated its age. The two men were moving the large compressor for the sandblasting apparatus into place, and arguing about which direction to take it. Bob was clearly anxious for them to get on with it so that he could send them on to the next job. He'd climbed down to the dam and asked me to come over to the machine so that he could demonstrate how the nozzle worked, and how to refill it with sand. He also showed me the general technique I should use. While he was showing me the protective headgear, one of the men thought recognized me.

"Are you Lance?" he asked.

"No. I'm Kevin," I replied.

"You look like Lance Carter. Where do you live?" he asked.

"I'm staying at Gene's place for now," I said, getting suspicious.

"Gene's an awfully good friend of mine." Bob piped in. "Always willing to help people in need. Now come on guys, we gotta get moving!" He wiped the sweat from his brow with a kerchief and said, "I'll be back at five to pick you up."

He and the two men scrambled up the ravine wall, tumbling rocks as they climbed. The man that thought he knew me peered back at me over his shoulder when he reached the top of the bank with an icy look. Then they climbed into Bob's truck and drove away. Once the noise of the engine faded, a silence surrounded me in the ravine. Cricket song and the occasional caw of a black crow were the only sounds to be heard.

I spent hours that day toiling in the heat. I had to contort my body in effort to reach awkward parts of the dam while holding the heavy sand hose. The work pushed my weak physique to the limit. Finally, I completed stripping the rust. I was totally exhausted. I sat down on the bank under a large oak, to cool off in the little bit of shade. My ears rang from hours of the compressor's loud and steady pulse. I had no idea of the time but assumed it was close to five. The area was stark, serene but lonely. The only company I had was the oak and the crow that perched on its branches. Since I didn't have my white powder friend with me, I anxiously looked forward to our meeting that evening.

The long, unbroken pitch of a vehicle horn sounded from above, disturbing both my thoughts and the tranquil setting of the ravine. I rose to my feet and began to clamber up the steep embankment. When I reached the top, a green truck with a white top that I did not recognize was waiting at the end of the dirt road. It had two occupants, one of which stuck an arm from the open window and waved. As I walked toward the truck, I recognized the two men inside as those who'd set up the equipment earlier that morning.

"Bob asked us to pick you up and take you back," one said laughing.

"You seem like you need a lot of help. It looks like a stiff wind would knock you on your ass." The other said with a laugh. "Jump in the back. We don't have all day!"

I climbed into the open bed of the truck as the two mocked me. The driver punched the gas in reverse and tossed me into the cab. Then the truck lunged forward and flung me against the tailgate as it skipped over the uneven dirt road. A cloud of dust consumed the bed and filled my lungs. Once on the paved road, the truck raced as if trying to outrun a fast-moving tornado. Keeping balance in the back of the pickup was impossible as the vehicle sped, weaving from one side of the road to the other. My thoughts raced in fear. What were they doing? Were they trying to kill me? Would I make it back unscathed? Finally, the truck slowed as we approached the drive leading up to the ranch house and then abruptly stopped.

"Here ya go!" The driver announced through his laughter.

"Thanks for the ride," I said sarcastically as I hopped out, my heart still pounding wildly in my chest.

"When you gonna get some food in ya? We could stick a post up your ass and you could be the scarecrow for this here place!" The driver said as he stuck his head from the window.

I walked past the vehicle and heard their laughter emanate from the cab. I wanted to get out of there. I held a straight line and continued walking away from the truck. As I walked my uneasiness grew. I passed the ranch house, it was quiet and cast long shadows across the ground. I was tense, not only from the terrifying ride but from the tormenting comments from the men. When I got back to the safety of my spot beneath the citrus tree, I peeked over the stone wall and noticed the unmistakable white top of the truck parked out on the road. It appeared to be waiting. I felt an overwhelming urge to hide, but it was too late. They'd seen me.

"Hey, we thought we would keep you company! You left like you were pissed off at us!" shouted one of the men. They bailed from the truck and hurried over toward the wall. I froze, not wanting to provoke a chase or aggression. They scaled the wall in a hurry and approached me.

"What's up?" I asked, as calmly as I could. "Please leave —" before I could finish, one of the men grabbed me around the waist and tackled me. I was thrown to the ground. I tried to curl up to protect myself, but before I could, the other guy kicked the left side of my head right above my temple. The blow was hard enough to temporarily blacken my vision. An arm wrapped around my neck, and I was peppered with continued blows to my abdomen. I lost the ability to breathe. My ears rang but I could hear their laughter. I laid with my back in the dirt, gasping for air and struggling to regain my eyesight. They rummaged through my pockets but found nothing. Determined to take anything I had, they searched around the wall and under my tree. One of the men called to the other when he found my blanket. In it was the radio but luckily nothing else. The other marched back over to me and delivered another kick to my ribs. This time, I heard the unmistakable sound of cartilage and bone. The pain was immeasurable. I clenched my hands and desired to call out but my voice had been taken away.

The laughing faded with their presence as they back-tracked over the wall. I lay there in the dirt writhing in pain. The vision in my left eye was coming back, albeit slowly. My right eye was still obscured. Every inhalation was excruciatingly painful, especially in my upper left side. I continued to lay on the ground. Getting up was impossible. The late afternoon light bled away, and I felt I might go with it. There was no one there to help me. No one to hear what happened or to soothe my pain. The trees above me remained silent and motionless, like my parents these last five months. I did not move for the rest of the night, the cool dark soil beneath was the only thing supporting me.

21.

THREE DAYS HAD passed since Bob's workers gave me the beating. The pain continued, particularly in my left upper quadrant, and was especially bad during deep respiration. The days were challenging but the nights proved even more so, as it was impossible to find a comfortable sleeping position. A local radio channel helped to fill my nonambulatory hours with popular shows like *The Shadow Knows* and Orson Wells classics. The summer heat proved to be a Godsend, it allowed me a certain degree of warmth and comfort during the nights. The covey of quail friends I'd acquired continued to delight my fragile spirit as they frolicked between the trees. My good fortune continued as I was supported by the wealth of oranges that surrounded me and Gene's kind offer to allow me to continue to stay at the far end of his orchard.

That afternoon, I heard the faint sound of voices coming from the ranch house. I watched for activity in the area and immediately recognized Bob's small frame by his unmistakable limp. He was headed in my direction. The quails were keen to his approach and fluttered away to the far side of the orchard field.

"Hey, young fella. I owe you some money," he yelled as he waved from a distance. I struggled to sit up. He kept coming my way. When he got closer to me, he noticed the bruising on my face.

"What happened to you? Did you have an accident?" he asked with sincere concern.

"Those two guys working for you beat me up after they dropped me off," I replied, laboring to speak. Bob crossed his arms and gazed off into the distance.

"Damn it. One of them is the son of a good friend of mine and I told him I would give his boy a job. I knew from the beginning he was trouble. You don't have to worry about them anymore. Are you okay? You look like you are having a rough time."

"I don't know. I think they broke a few ribs. I can sit up and I am starting to walk so I think I must be getting better," I said.

"When you're up and about, you let me know. I could use you for some more work. In the meantime, you rest up," he said as he handed me a check. He turned and walked a few feet before he stopped and repeated the question he had asked once before.

"I know it's none of my business, son, but don't you have any family? You know, kin who can take you in? I mean, being out here for so much time has got to get to a person." I found it difficult to make eye contact with him as I replied to his question.

"My parents divorced a while ago and I don't think either my father or mother really want me around. I think I've become a nuisance to both of them." My words arrested him and he said nothing for a moment. He was at a loss for a reply. At that moment, I felt awkward and embarrassed.

"I'm sorry young man. I'll see what I can do. You just rest up now," he said as he turned and walked away.

Uncontrollable tears welled in my eyes in response to the words that I'd spoken. Saying aloud how I felt after trying to hide my emotions for so long shook me. After a few minutes, I dried my tears and looked up, the covey of quail had reconvened close to where I was sitting. They were unphased by my presence. As the birds moved in harmony with one another, a sense of contentment rose in my heart. I looked up at the oranges clinging to the trees above, sunlight bathed their bright skins and I felt comforted. I closed my eyes and basked in this moment of peace. To me, the last ten minutes of my life had been comprised of a remarkable chain of events. I was fortunate to have Bob inquire about my well-being, to have all of the fruit above my head, its very existence sustaining mine, and the company of the quail to delight my heart. These unsung gifts buoyed my morale. If only I had the eyes to see, the true beauty of life was all around me. All I had to do was watch and listen. This day marks a pivotal point in my life. I'd learned one of the greatest lessons, partly from the pipe and partly in sobriety. No matter how low you get, there is always the opportunity to appreciate the small gifts that life gives you.

I was interrupted from my sun-kissed bliss by the sound of a car approaching. I peaked over the wall and noticed a white-topped vehicle. It had stopped a few yards from where I was sitting. I was immediately over-come with panic. The quail must have sensed danger and abruptly rose in the air to fly to a safer location. I froze in hopes that I would not be noticed. The hot air felt like it was pressing in around me. Then I heard a familiar voice.

"Hey, Kev. I wanted to come find you. I have a few other connections for you." It was Jules, who I hadn't seen since last Friday. He'd arrived in his old white pickup truck. He'd climbed the wall and was en route to my position before I thought to let the air I'd been hold-ing slowly escape my lungs. I was awash in relief. The anxiety slowly and smoothly drained from my body like lies from the mouth of a politician.

"Hey, buddy. How are you doing?" I asked quietly, it was still painful to speak.

"Goddamn, what happened to you?" he asked with surprise as he came close enough to see the trauma on my face. He sat down next to me and I told him of the events of the last few days.

"What a bunch of assholes! Are you feeling better?" he kindly inquired. I hesitated and then picked my words carefully, each sentence was a new experience of pain.

"I think so. It's slow for sure. At least I can see out of my eye now," I answered.

"I can introduce you to guys that will probably buy all of the smack from you. You should be able to move it all at once," he said, changing the subject. Jules snapped his fingers and asked, "Do you think you can make it if I take you to see them now?"

"Yeah, I guess I have to. I gotta meet those biker guys in a few days and they're gonna want their money. Give me a second," I said as I rose slowly.

It was three o'clock in the afternoon, three days after the beating when I finally got the impetus to get up and get going again. I had Jules help me remove the brown bag with the bundles from a tree limb where I'd hidden it. I labored over the wall with Jules' help and got into his truck with the elegance of a lumbering sea cow. We headed east down the road toward the foot of the Topa Topa mountains.

"I met this woman a few days ago. She doesn't really talk but seems really cool!" Jules shouted abruptly as if he'd been waiting to share his excitement with me. The uneven road narrowed into one lane. I cringed and sharply sucked in air with each bump and jolt. The pain in my ribs referred throughout my entire body. Oak leaves covered the pavement and the trees grew denser as we neared the mountains.

We arrived at a modest driveway that had a 'NO TRES-PASSING' sign on a small wooden post off of the main road. We turned down the drive and followed it until we reached a small Quonset hut surrounded by grand old oak trees, their age evident by their great girth. Rudimentary curtains hung from the hut's small windows and there was a crusty little welcome mat at the foot of the front door. An elderly woman emerged as we pulled up to the house. She had dark skin on her face, etched with years of deep lines, each with a story to tell. Her eyes were a vivid, light blue color. She had high cheekbones and grey hair tied up in a bun atop her head. She wore a long dress of brightly colored, thin fabric. She reminded me of a figure from Millet's famous painting, *The Gleaners*.

"Hey, Beatrice. This is my friend Kevin. He has the stuff you were asking about. Is now a good time?" Jules asked as we stepped from the truck. She nodded but remained silent, assessing whether or not to trust me. After a moment, she extended her hand to greet me and a slight smile crept across her face. I guess I passed. Her hand was cool to the touch and covered with dark pigmented spots. She turned and walked back into the hut, motioning for us to follow. Once inside, I noticed the walls were lined with shelves that held a large collection of books. There was a worn upholstered chair and a couch covered with cloth tapestries. A thick aroma of juniper lingered in the room. Beatrice sat carefully in a small chair at one end of the room, opposite of the couch where she gestured for us to sit. There were thickly braided rugs covering the wooden floor, their once bright colors had faded to a faint memory. Jules turned to me and pointed at the bag.

"She wants to take a look at it," he said. I stood up gingerly and handed her the bag. She carefully opened the bag and removed one of the bundles. Her speckled hands carefully unfolded the paper that disclosed its contents. She then wetted her index finger, touched the snow-white powder, and brought her finger back to her tongue to taste it. A pleasant smile arose on her face, it was a sign of her approval. Still, she'd said nothing. Each movement she made was deliberate and communicated her intent. She stood slowly, walked over to a little nightstand, and opened its top drawer. She carefully fished out a small cloth pouch.

"I think she wants it all," Jules whispered to me. She looked first at Jules and then at me. Then she opened the pouch. I got the feeling that she had information that I did not. Like she knew something about me or recognized me from the past, but I was uncertain. Something about her presence was comforting, yet unfamiliar. She quietly handed me a wad of money, the amount for the entire bag of heroin, with an air of grace. Wisdom seemed to seep from her piercing blue eyes. I wanted to know this woman.

"I have to get going. My mom wants me to finish mowing the lawn," said Jules, breaking the silence. We rose from the couch, and Jules led us to the door. Beatrice never broke her gaze on me. She stepped to one of the shelves and reached for a faded blue-covered book. She clasped it with both hands and looked longingly at me before extending it in my direction. I looked down at its cover, *The Tao* by Lao Tzu.

"Is this a gift?" I asked. She said nothing, but turned and walked slowly back to her chair. She sat and gazed out of the small window across the hut. It seemed as if she hadn't a care in the world. Her facial expression was one of contentment.

On the way back to the orchard, I asked Jules about Beatrice. He told me that he was introduced to her about a month ago by a potter who worked in the east end of the valley.

"Nobody really knows much about her. Edwin told me she likes hallucinogens so I thought we would try to see if she would be interested and lucky for us, it worked out! For some reason, she found you interesting," he shouted over the noise of the Ford.

I held the book in my hands and though I was completely unaware of its contents, I considered it something special. As the years passed, I'd read those pages time and time again. The words in that blue-covered book helped me through many turbulent times. Though that book has long since left my possession, the smell of that little Quonset hut remains with me to this day, much like the impressions of Beatrice.

22.

THE FALL OF 1974 nonchalantly replaced the oppressive summer heat with cooler nights. My sole wool blanket was no longer cutting it. I had a difficult time keeping warm. I felt like the goat on Evergreen Drive. Fortunately, my injuries had healed and all that remained of the beating weeks ago was the occasional sharp pain. The covey of quail made their presence less frequently now as they were priming to head south. The trees above me were now barren of fruit. The thought of how I was going to survive the winter played in a constant loop in my mind, so I turned to my trusty friend, the pipe, to soothe any physical or mental discomfort that I felt.

I continued to read Beatrice's gift, and it unveiled many new concepts to me. Perhaps I'd had them buried deep within my psyche someplace, only to be conjured up by the words in *The Tao.*

I finally finished Bob's project. The dam was now painted a brilliant red and the two workers who'd levied their anger on me had long since been dismissed from employment. As the months passed, Bob continued to hire me on occasion for odd jobs.

As the summer dwindled, I saw Jules less frequently. He'd found other people to hang out with that shared his mechanical interests. I seldom encountered him these days, but on one chance meeting, he told me that his mother had asked him to leave the house. He'd planned to leave the Ojai Valley and move up to the large metropolitan area of Los Angeles where he could find more opportunities to become an automobile mechanic.

I stopped in to see my mother on occasion. One fall afternoon I made a visit to her apartment. The yellow Fairlane station wagon was parked outside so I gave a quick knock on the turquoise front door. A minute passed before it opened.

"Well hi," she said, opening the door with wet hair. "I just got out of the shower. Come on in and make yourself comfortable."

"How have things been?" I asked.

"Oh, I don't know. My diabetes has been out of control and your father is still not sending his monthly checks. He is really something. The court ordered him to pay me monthly alimony and he refuses to do so. I could have him thrown in jail you know!" she exclaimed, exacerbated. She continued to rant, her anger and frustration obviously ran deep. She feared not getting financial support from my father or the state. The longer I stayed during our visits, the more clearly she became agitated. "You can't be here too long," she said. "I don't want the social service people to see you here. I could lose my benefits."

"I just wanted to stop in and see how you were doing," I'd say on my way out of the door. She'd always tell me to stay in touch as I'd leave. But I could feel that familiar sense of embitterment towards me. I didn't feel like a son, I felt like an uninvited guest. I was nothing more than a person who put her financial support at risk. That fall, my mother became more of a person that I used to know, than my mother.

Weeks continued to pass. I awoke one cold morning with frost glistening on the citrus trees. My limbs were stiff and my feet were numb from the cold. *The Tao* lay next to me with its pale blue cover, and the candle I'd used to read its poetic insights the night before had melted down, leaving a pile of wax in the dark soil. My mind went to Beatrice. I desired to see her again. I was uncomfortable visiting uninvited, but I felt an intrinsic yearning pulling me towards her Quonset hut. I decided that today was the day. I collected myself and put what heroin I had left in my pocket and scaled the wall. The early morning traffic was scarce and the few deciduous trees growing on the valley floor signified the arrival of the season by displaying showy, brilliant hues of yellow and orange.

After an hour of walking, I reached the end of Beatrice's drive. Fallen oak leaves were strewn all around the hut when I entered the yard. My footsteps were marked by the sound of them, quietly rustling underneath my feet. There was a hammock hanging in the yard, red and yellow leaves had begun to brown atop the cotton dura cord, suggesting that it had not been used in many days. The front step creaked as I approached and leaned in to knock on the door. There was no response. I sat on the small wooden front step with my back to the door and waited. The yard had a feeling of tranquility and peace, it was compellingly relaxing. Sitting on Beatrice's front stoop was more like retiring after a hard day of labor, rather than waiting for a particular action or encounter to take place.

Soon, I heard the sound of leaves stirring and crunching underfoot. Beatrice appeared from behind the Quonset, emerging from its curved, corrugated metal walls. She wore a bonnet, reminiscent of a pioneer woman, that cast a shadow over most of her face. A long buttoned burgundy dress covered her body. Over the top of the dress, she wore a pretty little blue apron. She did not act at all surprised to see me. In fact, her behavior indicated that she had been expecting my arrival. She stopped, stooped, and placed a small bundle of herbs that she held on a wooden tree stump and gestured for me to come to where she stood. She picked up a single stem from the herb bundle and slowly tied it into a little knot. On one end of the stem, there were a few very small, sepia-colored leaves. She continued tying the stem. Once she had tied six knots, she held it to her cheek and then blew on it, the small leaves fluttered to the ground. She then

reached toward me, placed the stem in my hand, and closed my fingers around it.

I pulled a bundle from my pocket and asked if she would like to join me. She

waved it off with her hand and walked back towards the hut, glancing at me as she walked. I couldn't determine if she wanted me to follow. But when she stopped at the door and waited, I realized then that that was my invitation. I followed her into the small room and the familiar fragrance of juniper delighted my senses. I walked toward the quilt-covered couch but she gestured for me to sit on the floor instead. She pointed to the floor at the end of the braided rug closest to the door. I sat nonchalantly and leaned back onto my arms to support my upper body. The stem that she gave me was still in my hand. Then, Beatrice sat down beside me and demonstrated a sitting posture, legs crossed with a tall, straight

back. I found this position
uncomfortable at first. Within five minutes, my back
began to ache, particularly the
left side where I'd sustained broken ribs just a month
ago. She took her hands and pushed my legs closer together in effort to correct my posture. My back pain
began to subside, but not entirely.

I sat motionless for what seemed like an hour. I
was unaware of Beatrice's presence thereafter. I looked
around the hut from my seated position but she was nowhere to be found. I was unsure if I was to stay on the
floor like this, or get up and leave. I began to feel uneasy.
I took the small stem she'd given me and started to roll
it back and forth in my hand.
Another hour passed, and then I heard a soft muttering
outside of the metal walls, but I could not discern what
it was. It didn't sound like voices or an animal and it
continuously changed in volume. The sound persisted
but kept moving from location to location. At one point I
thought it was coming from directly behind me. I turned
around on the rug but there was nothing there. Her expression was fixed and her movements were determined.
She strode past me to the opposite corner of the room.
I watched with interest as she reached for a small faded
paper envelope perched high on a shelf. She brought it
down slowly, her small darkened hands holding it carefully. Then she sat in the small fabric-covered chair and
opened the envelope, extracting what looked to me like
a small piece of white paper. On it were multiple tiny

printed faces, dark blue in color scrawled across the surface that was no larger than a quarter-inch in size. I started to get up from the braided rug but she quickly waved at me to stay put.

Carefully, she tore one of the small illustrated forms from the paper and then into a small rectangle. She fished a bit of cloth from the pocket of her apron and wrapped the piece of paper with the illustration inside. She pressed the cloth firmly with her thumbs, while softly moving her lips. Not surprisingly, no sound came out, but I was captivated by the movements of her deeply lined mouth. I watched her with curiosity and fascination. A few minutes passed, then she rose from her chair and walked over to me. Once again she reset my legs, this time with more firmness. She emphasized the posture that she expected me to maintain. Next, she unwrapped the cloth, picked the piece of paper up with her thumb and index finger, and brought it to my mouth. Instinctively, I wanted to take the piece from her but she pulled her hand back, grinning, as I reached for it. She opened her mouth and placed her tongue on its roof, gesturing for me to do the same. As I did, she gently placed the small piece of paper under my tongue. After that, she rose to her feet and motioned to me to remain on the rug. Then, she walked slowly to the little sink in the corner of the hut and gathered what looked like a bunch of green onions. I was unsure what was happening but I continued to watch intently. She began to braid the long green ends of the onions. After completing this task, she placed them on my right side and walked to the rear of the hut and out of sight. Silence befell the room. By now, I felt awkward. My legs had been crossed for far too long. I strained to remain still but found the posture to be increasingly uncomfortable. My arms seemed to lengthen and I was sure that I could reach out and touch the door from where I sat. The corrugated metal walls of the Quonset hut began to straighten. I sensed ripples running through my entire body, yet I remained relaxed, aware of my surroundings. I glanced toward the window to my left and noticed the largest crow I'd ever seen perched precariously on the small sill. It looked at me intently. It called to me and I understood its feelings precisely. The crow's size was already enormous, but it continued to grow and take up space in the window. I watched in amazement as its beak formed tangible words.

I then felt the sensation that my face had elongated. It was not a displeasing feeling, but it was rather foreign. I maintained the posture Beatrice set me into the best of my ability, but I felt like I was sitting on something fluid, rather than the solid floor. I struggled to maintain my balance. Shortly thereafter, I experienced forward movement, as if something was pushing me from behind. The door to the hut opened and I felt the urge to pass through it. The crow called to me, and I realized that it was directing my every thought. Beatrice reappeared and stood squarely in front of me. Her presence did not alarm me but had a soothing effect. I released the tension in my body. As I studied her, her body stretched and her head grew exceedingly long, and she began to move rhythmically in sequenced steps. Her arms moved along her sides and her fingers bent in contorted positions. Her lower lip dropped to show her teeth. The crow now seemed to be conducting Beatrice's movements. The dance was beautiful, all of Beatrice moved in unison, harmoniously. My eyes went back to the crow on the sill. It had filled the window entirely and blocked the light from streaming in. Then it began swinging its beak to and fro, from one direction to another before it opened its wings and took flight. When I turned back to Beatrice, she'd vanished.

The crow landed in the doorway of the hut, paused briefly, and then hopped deliberately in my direction. Its large mass was alarming, but I remained unruffled. It bounced to my right and gathered in its beak the braided onions lying on the floor next to me. It stopped momentarily, gazed deeply into my eyes, and flew out of the door and into oblivion.

From that point forward, things were unclear. The last thing I remember was lying on my right side cloaked in the darkness of the hut. When I came to, my eyes were slow to adjust. With great effort, I noticed a dim light a short distance from where I lay. In the light, recognizable images began to assemble like pieces of a jigsaw puzzle. They came in a specific order, and eventually formed a full picture of my reality. The light grew brighter and now illuminated the interior of the Quonset hut. I could then make out specific objects - chairs, books, and a small table. My hair and clothing were wet. I lay there on the floor for hours. My reference of time had been obscured. I sensed that it must have been past midnight by the time I finally peeled myself from Beatrice's floor.

The hut was engulfed by a heavy silence. The sensation of my body weight was considerable. My joints felt compressed by every movement. Beatrice was physically absent but I sensed the heart and soul of her all around me. Then, I heard a muffled sound. It was soft but distinguishable. It had rhythm and was familiar to me. As it grew louder, I recognized it as the same soft muttering I'd heard earlier that day, but I could not place its source. I stepped over the threshold of the front door and out into the night. The noise befell me like rain falling from the sky. Though I still could not determine the source of the noise, it was perceptible and I felt safe. I walked away from the hut, and as I did, the muttering noise faded and dispersed into the night sky. All became quiet again. I decided to head for the orchard.

Starlight proved sufficient to guide me on my journey. As I walked, I contemplated the strange experience and tried to decipher what I'd been shown. I had a new-found appreciation for life. Somehow, the experience had opened my heart, and I was able to accept things for the way they were, rather than wish for life to give me something different. I noticed small miracles and marveled at the fundamental truths which had been shared with me, like how to give thanks for all of life's riches. All of this I learned from an unsuspecting, beautiful, but mysterious old woman.

23.

IT WAS THE first week of September. I intended to enroll in the Nordhoff High School, more for the purpose of part-time food and shelter than for scholastic endeavors. I had been told by a substitute teacher, who I had recently done some lawn work for, that if I attended school full-time, the state would offer me, as an underprivileged kid, a free meal program. A few weeks before fall semester was to begin, I went to the enrollment office.

"You are a few weeks late to register!" the office lady fussed. "Please fill out this enrollment card and return it to me," she said in an annoyed tone. The information that the card requested was straightforward and brief. I filled it out to the best of my ability, until I reached a question that specifically asked for a parent or guardian. I paused to think about what to put and then listed Jules' mother.

I went back to the office and slid the registration card across the counter. As the registrar stood there with her back to me, I felt a brief pang of guilt. I had lied on the registration form. If I were to be found out, would I lose the benefits that I so desired? She turned around and looked the form over. Then, she peered over the top of her dark-rimmed glasses and sighed.

"Thank you. Please glance through this booklet and bring it back with the classes you wish to take." I completed the list in fifteen minutes and returned to the registrar's office once again.

"Thank you, have a good day," she said in a monotone voice without looking up from her typewriter. I was awash with relief when I stepped from the office. She hadn't questioned a thing. The walk back to the orchard took an hour. When I got there, I climbed over the old stone wall to my little spot under the citrus. My sole friend, the pipe, was waiting there for me, so I decided to take myself to a place of euphoria in celebration of the day's accomplishment.

School was relatively mundane. I had little interest in the subjects being taught, and the invitingly warm temperature of the classrooms encouraged slumber. I was often reprimanded by teachers for sleeping. On days when there were few classes, I lounged in the library, taking advantage of the comfort of central heat, or I went to the school gymnasium for a shower. I was desperate for a means to keep up my personal hygiene. School lunch was always a welcome treat and was my primary source of nutrition now that the citrus trees were barren.

One afternoon, as I was taking my lunch tray to the wash bin, I felt a hand pat me on the back. "Hey, is that you Meehan?" I turned to address the greeter and immediately recognized the face.

"Norman! How goes it? You decided to let your hair grow down to your shoulders I see. I didn't think your parents would let you do that!" I said laughing.

"I heard that you were killed in a car crash, man," he said with surprise. "Where are you living? You look like you've been on a diet or something. Get back to the counter and get some more food!"

Comments like Norman's left me with a tremendous sense of shame. I am unsure why I felt that way, even to this day, but I attribute it to the embarrassment that I felt when my peers pointed out my withering frame.

"I'm kinda camping out for now. I really like being outside," I said.

"Are you kidding? In this weather? You're nuts Meehan. Where's Steve?" Norman asked.

"He's still in Oregon but he's planning to come back soon," I answered. We walked from the cafeteria and outside to a small gathering area under a large sycamore tree. The day was crisp and the sky cloudless.

"I've got a connection on a lid, ten dollars and it's not shake. It's good stuff", Norman whispered as he leaned over to me.

"Do you know anyone looking for smack?" I asked abruptly.

"You're pushing that? That's hard stuff man," he responded with surprise. "I know one guy that might be interested. My brother Dave works with him at the hospital. He is the head of maintenance or something like that over there. I'm really not sure. Let me ask Dave. He should be out of class soon." Sycamore leaves fell from the trees around us, as we visited for a while longer, catching up on trivial things like girls and music.

"There's Dave! Hold on a second," Norman said as he hopped up and jogged over to his brother who was walking with a few other students. Norman caught up to his brother and he and his friends stopped in a small huddle. I watched with alertness while they talked in hushed voices since I knew the repercussions of getting caught selling drugs on campus. There were rumors that narcotic agents, narcs, had been placed on campus by the body of teachers. My physical appearance alone invited suspicion that I was into drugs. After a few minutes, Dave jogged back over to me, his long hair swaying from side to side. Short of breath, he related to me what was discussed.

"He told me he would talk to the guy and see if he is interested. Dave wants some though. What do you want for it?" I gave Norman the price per bundle and a meeting place if he was interested.

"Meet me here on Monday at this time. Can you do that?" he asked.

"Yeah. But I'm not going to carry," I said. "We've gotta do this off-campus." Then the bell sounded for class. Norman threw on his backpack.

"Let's catch up after class."

I had an open period so I stayed to keep company with the sycamore tree. I laid down on my back and looked into the light blue sky. My thoughts drifted to my brothers. I had hoped that the overwhelming abuse and negligence we had experienced together had diminished for them, at least for a while. I felt a sadness that extended across the thousand-mile distance that separated us. I hoped that they were all well.

The days were getting shorter and I still had not left the orchard. The sunlight faded much earlier now, taking the warmth with it. My Pendleton blanket had become incapable of keeping my thin body warm. I woke up to another morning of frost on the rich California soil. This meant that the wind machines located intermittently around the orchard, would soon be turned on. Large fans were used to move air around the trees so that frost would not accumulate and damage their fragile leaves. These fans thundered noisily, but I quickly became acclimated to the din of the machines. The ambient noise proved useful to lull me to sleep.

Smudge pots were also put out in lines between the trees like soldiers in formation. They were fueled by used sump oil and used for heat. As winter set in that year, my only source of warmth was the smudge pots that belched filthy black smoke. The pots created oily, dark clouds that lay thick on the valley floor and covered everything beneath them with soot. Nightly, I snuggled up to the broad base of a pot and watched the flame flicker inside the flue cap. In the mornings, my nostrils, head, and blanket were coated in a thick, oily black aftermath of a night next to a pot. Eventually, I developed a consistent cough, and hacked up gobs of repulsive dark mucus. The oil and soot that soaked my clothing day after day was atrocious. I felt defeated and I knew that I had better look for another place to live, at least through the winter.

I had not yet found another option for sleeping. Fallen eucalyptus leaves covered the ground behind the orchard where the train tracks once lay. Beatrice entered my mind and I had a yearning to go and visit her again. That familiar feeling of guilt and self-consciousness came up when I thought of dropping in unannounced. But I reasoned that it would not bother her, it was evident that she considered me a student. Surely her motivation to teach me had a certain purpose for her as well. Her ability to communicate nonverbally was, in itself, phenomenal. To me, she had re-defined my understanding of wisdom.

My footsteps quickened as I headed down the long drive to her hut. Would she be there, I wondered? It was five o'clock in the afternoon when I arrived at her doorstep. There was no movement inside the hut so, as before, I sat and waited on the well-worn, wooden front steps. The cold wind had stopped blowing. My eyes shifted over the area and fell to the left of the yard where small river rocks had been deliberately stacked to form what appeared like the beginning of a foundation for a small structure. I walked over to the rocks to assess in detail what I saw.

The stones were meticulously placed in a rectangular shape, the short end was closest to where I stood. Inside the stone parameter, there was a large pile of leaves. If this had been here before, it had gone unnoticed. Most people would overlook something as simple as this structure, but for some reason, I was deeply intrigued with everything in Beatrice's world. Without really thinking, I sat in the pile of leaves inside the structure at one end of the stones in the posture that Beatrice had shown me and waited.

An hour or so passed before I detected the movement of a figure on the road. Thick shrubs and oak trees made it difficult to get a clear visual. The figure paused and stood still for a few seconds and then continued on. It wasn't until the figure reached Beatrice's driveway that I could clearly distinguish a younger woman with long dark hair, wearing a shawl. I listened and detected the familiar muttering I had heard the last time I was here. The woman appeared to be deep in thought. She walked slowly but deliberately, muttering indiscernible sounds loud enough to be heard. As she moved the dim, dusk light hid the details of her face. Then, she disappeared behind a bank of thick shrubbery that lined the road. Everything became still, silent.

Fifteen minutes later, I sensed a presence behind me. I turned to see Beatrice walk up from the trees on the north border of the property. Her expression was firmly fixed. She strode directly for me. Her posture was slightly stooped, and her head seemed buried in the bonnet that she wore. When she reached the edge of the stone structure, she gestured for me to get up and out

172 ~ KEVIN MEEHAN

of it. I apologized and told her that I didn't mean to intrude. A forgiving smile flickered across her face. I asked if she had seen the young woman who had been walking up the road a few minutes ago. She turned and started back to the hut without responding to my question. I assumed I was to follow.

Dusk had turned to darkness. I went into the Quonset hut after her. It took a few minutes for my eyes to adjust to the darkness inside. There was one small night light in the corner. The smell inside was not the familiar juniper but something different. It was pungent, like the mothballs I remembered as a child in the depths of my parent's closet. Beatrice went to her little two-burner gas stove and placed a small cast iron pot on it. She adjusted the dial and a flame burst to life. She then reached high on the wall for what resembled a bota bag, a sheepskin water bottle often used by Basque sheepherders. She removed the small cap and held the bag over the pot. Dark liquid poured from it and into the pot which she held very briefly atop the flame. After the liquid was warmed, she poured it into three tiny, tan porcelain vessels which she set in a row, one next to the other. Then, she placed the vessels on a small wooden tray and carefully carried it to the front door.

I rushed to open the door for her. She passed by me slowly and I watched with curiosity as she delicately picked her way down the stairs and into the fallen leaves. Even in darkness, I managed to identify her movements as my eyes followed her to the stone structure. She stepped over the wall and into the interior. Carefully, she set the tray in the center and stood for what seemed like quite a long time, as if she was waiting for someone or something. I sensed that she did not want company so I stayed behind at the hut. I sat with my back to one wall, making an effort to pay attention to my posture. My lower back began to ache as the time passed and I began to feel restless and frustrated. I wondered if I should leave, did Beatrice have a plan for me tonight? Was there ever a plan at all?

The front door eventually creaked open. I had fallen asleep. Beatrice walked into the hut, tray in hand. It had now held only one porcelain vessel. She passed by me and set the tray on the wee table next to the upholstered chair. She picked up the remaining vessel and brought it to me. I started to stand up but she gestured for me to remain seated. I took the vessel from her hand and held it, glancing down at its contents. I could see only muddy-colored liquid. I brought it to my nose to smell it, but it had no definitive smell. It was simply dark and thick, like molasses. I glanced up at Beatrice, waiting for instruction. She went again to the shelf where she'd previously retrieved the envelope and stood on her toes. Again, she withdrew a tiny piece of paper and then tore a marked square from its corner. She walked to me with her hand extended, the square perched on the tip of her index finger. This time I placed it under my tongue myself. She indicated that I drink the fluid after I placed the square into my mouth. When I drank the solution,

I noticed that it tasted like the cough syrup my grand-father gave me as a child. Once again, she squatted in front of me and pushed my already crossed legs closer together with force. I held the position as she exited the room.

It was difficult for me to determine the amount of time that passed before I noticed the muttering. It started slowly and came from behind me, outside of the Quonset. In the dim light, I noticed a small blue-bellied lizard that had entered the hut. And I watched with inter-est as it moved along the corners of the wall. It stopped occasionally to lift its belly from the floor and then it moved on another few feet and repeated this movement. Beatrice was nowhere in sight, so I continued to focus on the lizard. It moved to the center of the room, directly in front of me about three feet away. Then it turned and faced me, motionless. Neither of us broke eye contact. We engaged in a silent standoff for what seemed like an hour, during which I began to feel deeply connected to it. The lizard's mouth began to move as if it was attempt-ing to talk. Then, it spun in a quick circle and stopped, looking at me squarely in the eyes. It did it again. This continued for a while until I decided that it must want to play. I lifted myself and laid face down on the floor. I spun around as the lizard had done. It took off to the far end of the hut and then looked back at me, so I did the same. We continued this game of copycat for hours until I felt physically exhausted and laid down on my back.

I stared up at the curvature of the hut's ceiling. As I was looking at it, the curve began to flatten, similarly to the way the corrugated metal wall had flattened. Then, I felt a heavy pressure on my lower abdomen. I looked down and saw the lizard perched on my torso, staring directly at me. Its mouth again started to open and close, but this time I heard sounds. They were soft sounds, like that of a small wave lapping against the hull of a boat. I was transported to a distant memory of a bell, ringing methodically as it woke me from sleep. I snapped out of it when a shadow cast by something passing through the street light walked by the window in the door.

I asked the lizard, "What do you want from me?" It stayed perched on my chest, looking to one side, as if it had spotted an insect to eat. I observed the dramatic blue on its belly that glowed like it was under a fluorescent light. All of the sudden, it skittered towards my left ear. I think it intended for me to hear what it had to say. I heard the wave sound again, this time more loudly than before. Its tiny claws gripped my clothing as it leaned closer to my ear. Waves lapped into memories. It was summer, the hay fields were dry, I was drawing under eucalyptus trees, warm Santa Ana winds blew on a lovely evening.

The lizard began to feel heavy. It felt as if a hundred-pound weight was sitting on my chest and I became quite uncomfortable. It must have sensed my discomfort because, lucky for me, it leapt from my chest and onto the floor. It spun again and I decided to restart the game.

We imitated one another on the floor of that Quonset hut until sunrise. When dawn approached, I was completely exhausted and drenched in sweat. I fell asleep on the floor.

Shortly thereafter, I awoke. I was surprised to find myself in the same sitting position where Beatrice had left me. My throat was dry but my body did not ache as it typically did when in the same position for an extended period of time. There was no one around, no sound, except for the muttering coming from the direction of the stones in the front yard of the hut. I slowly stood from my sitting position and walked to the door. When I opened it, I immediately recognized the young woman from the previous night on the road.

She stood in the middle of the stone structure, stone still, with her back to me. Her arms were raised above her head as if she were stretching from a deep sleep. She wore the same shawl as the day before. I watched her intently until she moved. She turned slightly, gracefully stepped over the rock border and walked back to the drive. Her head was still as she floated away, disappearing behind the thick bushes that lined the road.

I left the steps of the hut and went to the stone square where the woman had been standing. The tray and the two vessels Beatrice placed on the leaves the night before were still in place. I peered into the porcelain containers, but they were empty. I glanced toward the road in search of the young woman, but there was no sign of her. Like Beatrice, she had vanished. The early morning sunlight suddenly darkened by rain clouds forming over the Topa Topa Mountains.

Some time passed before I heard rustling from the bushes behind me. It was Beatrice, she wore the same bonnet, and I thought it gave her an air of mystique. She moved past me and squatted to pick up the tray. When she stood, she looked towards the road as if something was there that I was not able to see. When she turned toward me, her expression said it all. She was so unlike anything from this world, yet she communed with the earth unlike anyone I'd ever met. Her eyes sparkled with insight.

I watched her keenly as she glided peacefully back to the Quonset hut. Just before she reached the door, she spun a slow circle and looked back towards me with a casual grin. Suddenly, I noticed the shawl she wore. I did not recall her wearing one before. But now I realized that it was the same one that the young woman had worn who'd stood in the stone square just moments before.

Little did I know at the time, there was an indescribable element taking hold in my life when I went to see Beatrice. I was learning the process of observing life for what it is, rather than what I wanted it to be. Beatrice's teachings were taking hold and budding inside of me. Life's truths were hidden deep, but would occasionally peek through my subconscious, like a small baby kit carefully watching to assure the safety of its surroundings before leaving its den. I could not stop smiling as I walked the lonely road back to the orchard. When I arrived, I lay one the ground and fell immediately to sleep. I was physically tired but emotionally enlivened.

24.

IT WAS MID-NOVEMBER, 1974. I had been fortunate that the weather had been relatively dry up until this point, which had saved me from the laborious task of finding a new place to shelter. The occasional rainstorms that had come through had been brief and the scant moisture had not been enough to penetrate the tree canopy that I slept under. Dips in nightly temperatures though were a different matter. Continual exposure to the oily soot emanating from the smudge pots had taken its toll on my respiratory system. My cough had gotten quite a lot worse. But I had grown mentally tough. I was used to the elements and felt at home in the orchard. Yet I knew through reasonable deduction that I would not be able to continue this unprotected lifestyle for very much longer.

It was Friday evening and once again, the particulars for the heroin exchange had changed. I was now to go to Soule Park, a relatively quiet location isolated from residential homes, and much closer to the orchard than the Mexican restaurant had been. The days had shortened and I waited in darkness for the arrival of the current supplier. A car had been substituted for motorcycles. It pulled in front of the gate that restricted the public from the park during night hours. Two men exited the vehicle, one I recognized, the other I did not.

"Over here!" I shouted as they searched the grounds in the dark.

"What are you doing out so late?" the familiar man asked, laughingly.

"How's it going?" I asked in a routine manner.

"Good kid. Listen, the cost has gone up on this stuff. I'm gonna need thirty-five a bundle. Our supplier got busted so our stash is getting low. You can still keep your personal stash though," he said.

My addiction had become so severe at this point that I had no other option but to agree to the terms of the price increase. I took the package from him and, as usual, agreed to meet back at the same spot in one week. Before I could turn to leave, the other man started asking me questions about where I was staying. I interpreted his inquiry as mere curiosity, so I relinquished where and why I'd been sheltering where I was. After a few minutes of trivial talk, we headed for the park gate. The men got in the car and drove off.

I walked along the road back to the orchard. My mind worried about the increase in bundle price and I wondered if my usual buyers would be able to afford the jump. I did not want to lose this gig. I wasn't worried so much about the hundred dollars a week that I earned for moving the smack, but about losing my personal cut.

Once I got back to the orchard and settled under my blanket snuggled close to the smudge pot that night, I visited with my old friend. As I filled the bowl, I thought about the old man who'd left it behind at the bus depot.

The glow from the powder intensified with my deep inhalation, and I wondered what kind of stories this pipe could tell? The stress in my body quickly seeped out of every muscle group, as if nimble fingers massaged away the tension. The worries of the world drifted away like cinders from a campfire and floated up towards the heavens. The coldness of the night air fell away and I drifted into a deep sleep.

I woke to the morning light and the vibrating sound of the wind machines. A low tulle-like fog hovered above the valley floor. It was thick enough that the trees on the far side of the orchard were obscured. My body felt cold and depleted. The damp chill in the air motivated me to get up and get to school. The warm building and a hot meal were especially welcomed on cold mornings. I removed a few bundles from the package that I picked up the night before and buried them deep in my pocket. I wanted to have them handy in case Norman or his brother decided to buy them. Even though I'd told Norman I wouldn't carry at school, I felt that I had to take the risk since I only had a week to sell at the elevated cost.

I walked the hour to Nordhoff High, and found the warmth of the homeroom well worth the effort it took to get there. I sat down at my desk and wished that I could stay there forever. A whisper came from behind me, then an extended arm with a note in hand. I took the note and unfolded it. In close to illegible cursive, it read, "Do you have any stuff on you today?" I turned to look behind me. Paul was there and gave me a nod. I nodded back. When the bell rang to dismiss class, I stayed in my seat until the last student left the room. When I finally got up, Paul was waiting for me a few feet outside of the classroom.

"What's up?" I asked as we walked down the hallway.

"The word is I can get some smack from you," he said.

"Yeah, thirty-five a gram. The supply has been knocked so the price just went up. It's eighty-plus percent pure and not cut so I think you'll be happy with it," I said.

"That's steep but I'll take a few," he said.

"Do you have the coin?' I asked.

"I can get it after school. Can you meet me at the bleachers, about four?" he asked.

I nodded and we parted ways. I had not seen Norman but assumed I would run into him somewhere that day. The subtleties of classroom comfort were taken for granted by my fellow classmates. Most longed to be home or engaged in other activities, but I lavished in the warmth of the school building. I often sat at my desk long after class had been dismissed. On this day, I sat at my desk after class until the clock on the wall indicated three-thirty p.m. I got up and headed for the bleachers. When I turned down the hall corridor that led to the gym, I quickly noticed two adults speaking to Paul outside of our meeting location. My instincts were correct, I should not have brought the smack to school. I pivoted and headed in the opposite direction. I didn't break my step until I'd walked all the way back to the orchard. I'd have to be a lot more cautious if I wanted to avoid the law. I suddenly felt stressed and overwhelmed. How was I going to get all of it moved before the end of the week? What would happen if I didn't?

School lunches were sustaining me, but just barely. I was still not consuming enough calories to fuel my growing teenage body. The hour-long walk to school and back along with night after night of shivering, resulted in my body burning far more calories than I consumed. I was still losing weight. I went to sleep hungry, I woke up hungry. Visits to my mother's apartment were less frequent, that food source had dried up. And the oranges had long since been harvested, their sweetness would not touch my lips for months to come. The smack was all that would satiate my appetite. I smoked it nightly to help me go to sleep.

I awoke that night in the orchard with an eerie feeling. I lay on the ground facing the smudge pot on my left side, listening for anything unusual. The flicker of flame from the flue cap and the constant noise made by the steady rate of the burning oil provided familiarity, security. It must be nothing, I thought. And I closed my eyes in an attempt to fall back to sleep.

Suddenly, a man's screeching shout struck me like a hammer. "Move and you're done kid!" I was filled with terror. I tried to move, to turn and look toward the voice but a hand held my head firmly to the ground. I could feel small rocks indenting the skin on my cheek. I felt something small and firm pushing into the mandibular notch of my jaw. It was cold, so I assumed it was a metal bar of some sort to strike me if I didn't cooperate.

"I'm taking your stash. Just lay there and deal, man!" he yelled in a panic.

He let go of my head and rushed around me in search of the smack. I turned my head enough to get a quick glimpse of a man holding a semi-automatic handgun. He pointed it at me as he scrambled around. His bare head shifted to and fro, glancing back at me every few seconds to make sure I hadn't moved. He found the bag of heroin in a tree and lunged back toward me, pressing the gun against my neck. His hands were shaking. I thought the time had finally come. My heart beat rapidly in my ears. It was going to end, here and now, for a young teen who should never have been. My physical and emotional suffering would finally be over. I felt like this was how it was supposed to be. Not a tear would be shed for the death of a forgotten boy, whose only desire had been to be wanted, loved, and accepted.

The rate of the man's breath increased, and I squeezed my eyes shut and waited. In an instant, he sprang to his feet and ran for the stone wall. I could not move. I stayed frozen for what felt like eternity next to that burning smudge pot. My heart continued to race, I went into shock. I stared up at the night sky in an attempt to comprehend the point of a life. It dawned on me that the man who'd just come was the same man from the exchange in the park a few nights ago. I laid there against the cold soil wondering, was I fortunate or unfortunate to have survived?

25.

BY THE END of November, rains had started to soak the valley floor. Keeping dry was my primary focus, as the citrus tree canopy no longer provided adequate protection from the moisture. One Saturday, drenched and downtrodden, I gave up the task of staying dry and headed for Beatrice's Quonset hut. Not only did I desire guidance, but I also desired shelter, at least for one night. I did not dare go to visit my mother. Her continued angst about social services discovering me in her residence was something I wanted to respect. The feeling of abandonment also kept me away. I knew that I was not wanted, and to be turned away repeatedly was more than I could bear.

When I arrived at Beatrice's, I noticed that the front wooden step had not been swept. Leaves were strewn deeply at the front door. I walked to the rear of the hut and found several small rugs, rolled and bound tightly with twine, stacked against the outer wall of the hut where they would not get wet. I recognized them as the rugs that had been laid out on the floor inside the Quonset. I knocked several times on the door but there was no response.

Deflated, I turned and walked back to the road. There, a short, stout woman with a long coat called to me from the neighboring drive. "If you're looking for Beatrice, she went to Arizona for the winter." I waved in thanks for the information. My disappointment was greater than I could have imagined. Where was I to go now? My mind ran through all of the possibilities I could think of for winter shelter. On my way to the hut, I'd passed several homes that produced the mild aroma of dinner and had the hushed sound of voices coming from within. The light that streamed from their interiors suggested comfort and warmth. Perhaps if I went back and knocked on doors, informing people of my predicament that maybe, just maybe, someone might offer me shelter.

With gallant bravery, I decided to tackle the challenge. Retracing my steps, I headed back down the road towards the homes that I had passed on my way to Beatrice's. One house after another, I made my plea only to be denied time and time again. Some people made threats toward me, others offered a good luck farewell. I persisted. I asked if I could sleep in garages just to get out of the rain for one night, but the refusals continued, and understandably so. My appearance spoke of untidiness and perhaps even distrust. Several homes in the area had experienced burglaries around that time and tensions were high among homeowners. When I hit Oak Street, I noticed a man working on a Jeep in the driveway. I slowly approached and said hello. He poked his head out from under the vehicle and returned my greeting. "You like Jeeps?" he asked.

"Yeah. I don't know much about them but I think they're cool," I said.

He slid out from under the car and asked if I wanted a soda. I accepted and thanked him. Then, he walked into the garage where two lawn chairs sat open. "Come on in. Where are you from?" he asked.

"I've been staying up on Grand Avenue," I replied.

"Yeah. Where at?" he asked. I sat down in one of the lawn chairs and gave him a brief rundown of my circumstance. Occasionally we were interrupted by his preschool-age children who kept going in and out of the door from the garage that went into the house. While we sat talking, the sky opened up and rain began to pour. I was grateful that a roof was over my head, if only temporarily. A time of idle banter passed before I mustered the nerve to ask him for shelter, if only for one night. He made me an offer. "Tell you what, you clean this place up, I'll let you stay in here for the night."

I gladly accepted, shook his hand and introduced myself.

"I'm Christian, the name couldn't be more appropriate," he laughed and carried on. "I'm an elder at the Kingdom Hall down on Tico Road." He informed me that he was a Jehovah's Witness and then pontificated on his religious values. I sat there quietly and listened, asking occasional questions to fane interest.

"You should come down sometime and take in what we are all about. Anyway, it's getting late and I'm gonna head into the house. If you want covers, there are some thick blankets up on that shelf. I'll close the garage door. If you have to take a pee, just head out that side door and you can go in the hedges," he said, as he stood from his chair. Then he was gone.

The sound of small children was punctuated by random crying and screaming. I went about cleaning the cement floor and placed rags into empty containers. After a few hours, as I swept the last of the fallen debris from the floor, I felt that my end of the bargain was complete. I then wrestled a few of the blankets down from the shelf and made a temporary bed on the garage floor. The rain was still coming down when I turned the fluorescent garage light off and laid down on the pile of blankets. My standards had become so low, that I felt rather princely lying on a stranger's garage floor out of the pouring rain. Sleep overtook me in a hurry.

I was awakened by light streaming from the door of the house. "Wanted to make sure everything was okay in here," Christian whispered from the door. "Hey, looks like you did a great job tidying up from what I can tell," he slipped into the garage and closed the door behind him.

"I want to tell you something, Kevin. I was in there thinking about how lost you are. You need to have Jehovah in your life, son. He cares about you and is hurting that you are living in squalor, young man. You know, it is a sin what you are doing by not having him present in your life," he said as he sat down next to me. "Do you like girls?" he asked.

"Yeah," I replied, uncomfortably.

"Well, now that too is a sin son, since you are not married and such. You shouldn't have those types of thoughts. I counsel a lot of young men like yourself about this. I want to give you a publication to read. It's called *The Watchtower* and it details a lot of things you may find interesting," he said as he set a pamphlet on the floor. The rain got louder.

"Do you like boys?" he asked, lowering his voice.

"No sir," I replied. I was becoming increasingly uneasy with his questioning.

"Well. You shouldn't judge something before you've tried it," he replied in a near whisper. After that, neither one of us spoke. The dreaded, heavy silence weighed on me for what felt like decades. "I counsel young men like you about this every day," he said as he crept closer. "Stay still, Kevin. I don't wish to hurt you, young man."

In a flurry, I tossed the blankets off and started for the side door of the garage. It was locked. It was dark, but not so dark that I could not make out objects. I anxiously searched for something to defend myself, but it was too late. In my hesitation, he'd lunged and gotten a strong grip on me. I struggled to free myself and broke loose. I went for the door to the house. Before I could reach it, I was struck in the back. I felt for the Jeep, but I couldn't see well enough to find it. I was hit again in the back, directly above my right shoulder blade but I kept moving, trying to get to the door.

"Come on son. The more you resist, the tougher this will be on you," Christian said, struggling to catch his breath. "We're going to make sure you find Jehovah now son."

Just as I reached the door, it was darkened by a figure blocking the entrance. I felt a sharp blow to my head as I stumbled back toward the jeep. My energy was running out. I didn't have the stores to put up a fight, It left my body like the sand from an hourglass. I groped across the floor, my ears ringing from the blow, for anything that I could use to fight back. At some point, several cans of gas got knocked over and filled the garage with the acrid smell of gasoline.

Another barrage of blows came from behind me, some missed their mark, others were successful in their attempt. I had no more energy to give. My limbs felt like rubber, and the pain intensified as my adrenaline diminished. I fell to my knees, as hopeless as when the gun had been held to my jaw. Sweaty hands grabbed at me, looking for physical reference points. I flashed back to the incident in the shack filled with sawdust. Only this time, I was fully conscious. He tore my pants from my body in uncoordinated movements and pinned me to the floor. I was unable to move much aside from slight inflections in my arms and legs. My body had quit me. It surrendered. I screamed, pleading for help, but to my surprise, no one came. The house remained still. He rubbed himself against my bare buttocks, and I could feel his sexual arousal against my back. I was repulsed. How could this be happening again? My mind was flooded by the horrific memory of the first time. Was I to blame for this?

He held me by the neck and shoulder and continued the act of sodomy in waves. It was the longest, most horrific fifteen minutes of my life. I went completely numb. I remember he said that he'd completed what Jehovah had wanted him to do. Then he left me on the cold cement floor and went back into the house with his wife and kids. He said nothing when he left. The physical exhaustion I felt was unbearable. I lay on the floor, listening to the sound of rain on the roof until I could muster the energy to move.

I managed to get to my feet and take small steps. I fished my soiled jeans from the floor and put them on. Sharp pains fired through my hamstrings with every movement. I attempted to go through the side door again, to no avail. I banged on it in hopes it would spring open. I kept turning and jiggling the knob, pleading for it to unlock and let me out of there. Finally, I headed for the lights and searched around the garage until I found a large screwdriver in a toolbox. With much effort, I managed to finagle the door open, and I was back out into the rain. Pain encompassed my entire body. I had the strength to walk away from that house, but I was unable to make the full journey back to the orchard that night. I stopped under the awning of the town bakery and crumpled to the ground. That is where I took my rest that evening. I went in and out of sleep for hours until I was roused by the bakery's janitor and told to leave.

I slowly continued my way back to the orchard. A man and woman walked toward me on the sidewalk and smiled gleefully as they approached. The woman carried a stack of pamphlets under her arm and extended her hand to give me one on her way by. She smiled as she handed me the folded piece of paper.

"Find Jesus, my young friend. Jehovah loves you," she said. I looked down at the cover, it was entitled *The Watchtower: A Wolf in Sheep's Clothing. How Jehovah Will Protect you.*

26.

THE CHRISTMAS SEASON came and went. The only things that indicated its presence were the outdoor lights that intermittently adorned homes en route to school and the lonely, half-empty candy dish that sat on the laundromat counter. I'd gone there one evening in hopes of removing the days of smudge oil and soot buildup from my clothes andwoolen blanket. Unfortunately, repeated washings failed to clean the blanket as the filth had become part of the woven fabric.

The desks in homeroom were half-empty on Monday morning when Norman leaned over to me on his way by my desk. "Meehan. Can we talk after class?" I nodded. I had become even more careless around the campus in regards to supplying smack to my fellow classmates. I am unsure if it was due to my desire to establish some sort of trust in humans, or whether part of me didn't care at all if I got caught. When the school bell sounded, I rose from my desk and headed to meet Norman.

"Man, I know things have been kinda hot lately with the narc they put on campus," he said nervously. His body displayed a fidgety mannerism, and he twitched periodically. "My brother and I are interested in getting a few grams from you," he said.

"Who were those guys with you the last time I was gonna set you up?" I asked, skeptically.

"I don't remember. That was a few months ago," he said. "Wait! Are you talking about the assistant coaches for the football team? One of the guys was bald, right?"

"What are you guys looking for? How many grams?" I asked, ignoring his retort.

"Give me a few. How about four?"

"Meet me down at Libby Park after school. Let's make it four-thirty. I don't want to deal this stuff on campus, you got me?" He agreed and walked away, calling out to a few of his buddies who were headed in our direction.

I had a history class to get to. Unenthusiastically, I headed to classroom number twenty-seven. The smell of chalk dust hung in the air. Half of the orange seats with wooden desks attached were unoccupied and out of order. They'd been scattered about by the previous class who hadn't put them back in rows. I chose a seat in the rear of the classroom for a couple of reasons. One, I didn't want to attract any attention, and two, I didn't want to be noticed. I lacked even a hint of self-confidence in the physical state I was in. I settled into a seat situated at the rear of the room. The topic of the day was the three branches of the United States Government. As the minutes drew out the teacher, Mr. Smitherman, drolled on about the legislative branch. He was interrupted by Mr. Letterman, the dean, who requested to speak to him with a hand gesture from the door. They had a brief huddle in the hallway and then Dean Letterman poked his head into the room and scanned the class. When his eyes landed on me, they stopped. He waved for me to follow him. So much for going unnoticed, I thought. When I got up from my desk, the room fell silent.

I followed the dean with curiosity. Have they found me out? Or was this summons in regard to something else? He did not speak until we reached the doorway to his office. The sky was a brilliant blue that day and snow-topped the Topa Topa Mountains in the distance. I hesitated to enter the office, something pulled at me. When I stepped into the room, two police officers stood waiting. Dean Letterman turned toward me abruptly and barked, "Tell us where you're getting the stuff you're selling! I've had student after student tell me that *you* are the supplier for all of the junk on campus! I will not tolerate this type of behavior, Meehan. Am I clear?"

"Yes sir," I replied sheepishly. I glanced in the direction of the officers.

"Where are you getting it?" he asked again. I hesitated before I answered, my eyes went to the dean who paced frantically up and down the office.

"It's left for me at a pick up location and I don't see who is leaving it. I get money for moving it, enough to buy food." The words fell awkwardly from my mouth. I was not a good liar.

"Okay, well I can't locate your guardians. Tell me how to do that," he said, frustrated. I responded slowly to his question. I told him where my mother's apartment was located and that I didn't know her phone number. He looked perplexed. I readied myself for more questions.

"You don't know your mother's phone number? You live in the same house. How can you not know her phone number?" he asked in an irritated tone. His suspicion mounted and his body posture bowed, indicating his determination to get answers. I hesitated again, wondering how much I should reveal. But, I was cornered.

"I haven't been living at her home. I've been staying in the orchard on Grand Avenue," I said, honestly. He reached for my file that sat on the desk in front of him.

"You reported that you were living with Mrs. Claymore on your registration card. When did this change?" he asked.

I hesitated again, my legs began to fidget. I told the dean and officers that my mother did not want to lose her benefits from social services and then I reiterated my previous statement.

"I've been living in the orchard."

"Selling junk *and* no guardian, is that right Meehan? Let me put it this way, you are in a whole heap of trouble! I'll leave it up to these officers to decide what to do with you," he said as he stormed from the room.

"I'm Officer Bryant. Stand up. I'm going to read you your Miranda Rights and then we're going to take you into custody," he said, as he cuffed my hands. After my rights had been read, I was escorted from the dean's office to a patrol car outside. The rear door was already open as if it had expected me. I was ushered into the back seat and immediately impressed by the comfort and luxury of the vehicle. The warmth inside the cruiser indulgenced my senses. Regardless of my future, at that time in the back of the cop car, I felt nothing but bliss.

The sound of the dispatcher's voice echoed on the radio while I waited for the two officers to go back into the school and get their paperwork. A small group of students gathered around the car, looking for a little entertainment to break up the monotony of yet another school day. After what seemed like half an hour, the officers came out of the building and made their way back to the patrol car, shooing away onlookers.

The car pulled from the school's parking lot and we started on the short trip to the local police department. "We're going to take you in and print you. At this time we don't know if we'll send you to the Ventura Detention Center or hold you here," said one of the officers as we drove.

I commented on the comfort of the patrol car, perhaps in an effort to ease the tension. The same officer turned and looked over his shoulder at me with a surprised expression. "Do you have any idea what's going on? You are being held in custody as a suspect for the distribution of heroin on a school campus." Both officers shook their heads in disbelief.

The duration of the ride was not long enough for me. I savored every second of comfort. We pulled in front of the Ojai Police Station entrance and the attending officer opened the rear door of the vehicle. I stepped out into the cold. The officer quickly escorted me inside and began the standard booking process for juveniles. I flowed from one fluorescent light to another. They took my fingerprints, mug shot and had me fill out multiple information forms.

The cop at the desk reviewed my papers and then joked with his secretary. "You going bowling this evening?" he asked her. Then he turned to me and casually gave me the rundown. "We're going to keep you detained here for at least a few nights and then see about sending you to the Ventura Center. Follow that officer and he'll take you to the room where you'll strip and be given your issued uniform." I did as I was told.

Fortunately, I was given a pistachio green-colored cell all to myself. The walls were enamel and glistened under the bright fluorescent overhead lights. In it, was a small louvered window covered by heavy metal screening that sat in the upper corner of the back wall. The cell was quite an improvement from the cold, damp soil that I was used to. There were two cots in the room. I sat on one and was immediately taken back to Evergreen Drive. The only difference was that the blankets on the jail cot were much more adequate, and the temperature in the cell was quite a lot warmer than that of my basement room.

I found it a challenge not to fall into the mindset that this would be a more preferable way to live. Shortly after I'd arrived, the door to my cell was unlocked and an officer directed me to follow him to the mess hall. There, two long cafeteria tables sat parallel to one another. The walls were painted a stark, yet inviting, shade of white. Two other jail mates accompanied me in the hall. I sat alone at the far end of one of the tables, with no desire to converse. Food was brought to us on plastic trays by an emotionless prison employee. The trays were identical to the ones used in the high school cafeteria. On my tray was a bowl of soup, a bologna sandwich, and a can of peas. I found the meal delightful and I couldn't believe my luck. I'd had the opportunity to eat a warm meal, in a warm room, before getting to sleep in a proper bed, with warm bedding! The guard gave us half an hour to eat our meal before we were each escorted back to our cells. That night was the most peaceful, restful, comfortable sleep I had experienced in months.

I woke the next morning to a knock on the cell door. There was an officer outside waiting to escort me to the mess hall. This was admittedly not my normal routine. I was not accustomed to eating more than once a day. The invitation to get up and have breakfast was a pleasant surprise indeed. Two other juvey inmates nodded out of courtesy when I got to the mess hall. We sat down to oatmeal and toast. I was warm and my belly was full for the first time since I could remember. All my life, society told me to stay out of jail. But now that I was in jail, it was much more pleasant than I'd been told. Three square meals and a warm bed was not a bad bargain if you asked me. After breakfast, I was escorted back to my cell where I climbed back into bed and immediately fell into a comfortable slumber.

Two hours later, I heard another knock on the cell door. This time, the security guard said, "Meehan, please step out of the cell. You have a call." I got up and followed him to a small room near the department's dispatching office. From there, I could see through the glass doors to the outside. Heavy drops of rain pelted the asphalt beyond the entrance. I was grateful to be indoors, sheltered from the deluge. The security guard stepped outside of the room but stayed within earshot when I answered the phone. "Hello?"

"Kevin, this is your mother. The police department called me last night and informed me that you have been arrested. Listen, honey, I think there is a way for you to be able to stay with me. I'll talk with the welfare department to see if they can register you as my dependent. I'm moving into another apartment. You remember Larry Thacher? He has a place for rent next to his house on Boardman Road. I went and took a look at it and there is a small loft you can sleep in. The police have told me that if I take you into custody, they will drop the charges because of your juvenile status."

I couldn't believe my ears. As I held the receiver, I felt a tremendous surge of emotion coarse through my body. The first thought that entered my head was to have shelter from the cold. Then, I wondered if mom actually wanted me? I had spent the last year absolutely crushed. I had only begun to implement the tools of survival that included mental fortitude and resilience. I did not know if I could risk losing it all again. The trajectory of my life shifted in that moment. I made a knee-jerk decision. Even if mom's offer fell through, *someone* had shown a desire to help. The fact that that someone was my mother, stunned me.

I hung the receiver back on the hook. "Your mother will be here to pick you up in a few minutes. Please come with me and we will return your personal articles," said the officer on duty. I got dressed in my filthy, tattered clothes, the same ones that I'd worn for more than a year now.

Shortly thereafter, the yellow Ford Fairlane pulled up outside of the glass doors. My mother got out in the pouring rain and hustled into the station. She had an attitude of optimism. I stood from my chair, and she gave me a firm embrace. Then, she asked the officer behind the desk what needed to be done in order for me to be released into her custody. She was escorted to another room and I was asked to remain in my seat.

Two hours passed before she returned. During that time I sat dumbfounded in the little waiting room off of the main entrance to the police station. Occasionally, other law-breaking citizens passed through the doorway, casting their shadows on the well-waxed floor that reflected the bright fluorescent lights from above.

When the door finally opened, I heard the voice of the detaining officer. "Now Mrs. Meehan, we expect you to assume full custody of your son at this time." He gestured for me to get up and step into the room where my mother sat at the end of a long table.

"Sit down, Kevin. I want you to understand that you are being released into your mother's custody at this time. She will be responsible for you from this point forward. She has been informed that if we hear of any other illegal activity on your part, you will be immediately detained and sent to the juvenile correction facility where you will wait for trial. Am I clear on this? The court magistrate has been extremely lenient with you and is trusting that you will abide by the law. You are to remain in school and the dean of Nordhoff High has been informed of this arrangement. I don't want to see you here again! Do I have your promise?" he asked sternly.

"Yes sir," I quickly replied.

PART 4
Boardman Street, Ventura County California

27.

MOM AND I left the correction facility and went to the apartment that she had arranged to rent. The rain had slowed for the time being and patches of blue sky peeked through the clouds. I felt hopeful. As the Ford's tires rolled down the wet streets, I was overwhelmed by the fact that family had come back into my life.

The old apartment was tucked behind a small rural farmhouse not far from the orchard I'd called home. There was a wooden carport that we pulled the station wagon under. I was soon to discover that neither it nor the apartment were structurally sound. When I walked through the narrow door that entered the apartment, there was faded green carpet reminiscent of the family room in the basement on Evergreen Drive. I was struck by the commonality of the material. There was a small loft to one side of the stairwell, with a ceiling height of no more than four feet, yet it felt like a kingdom to me. I drank in the feeling of being wanted, like a thirsty desert inhabitant stumbling into a precious spring deep within heat scorched sand dunes. But in my euphoric state, my brothers kept coming to mind. How were they doing and had their living situation changed since I'd left?

Soon after I moved into the apartment, I got the answer to my question. I opened the door one afternoon in response to a knock. "Hey, Steve! You made it!" I exclaimed excitedly at the sight of my older brother.

"Finally, right?" he replied.

"Come on in. How did you know where to find us?" I asked with interest.

"I found mom's number and she gave me the address," Steve said. I was elated that he had made it back.

"You can crash where I've been sleeping," I said.

"No, that's okay. I'm going to crash over at Dave's house for a while. Can I get some food?" he asked. I showed him to the kitchen. As he searched through the sparse contents of the refrigerator, I inquired about Pat, Tim, and Terry and all that had happened since I'd left.

Steve said that he'd left for Ojai shortly after I had. Terry departed the Evergreen Drive house about two months later. He'd moved in with an acquaintance of his from school. "Pat's having a real rough time. Lynn has taken most of their food away now. It seems like she's punishing them for you, Terry, and me leaving. It ain't good," Steve said. "I was thinking that if—" he stopped short at the appearance of our mother.

"Steven! My word, how are you? I'm so happy to see you," she said gleefully. "How are Pat and Tim?"

"Not good, Mom. Pat looks like a skeleton at this point," he replied.

"Well, I will see to that. I'm going to get both of them tickets to get down here ASAP," she said sternly. "Now come on in, and please stay for a while."

I lived with my mother for the entire year of 1974. That year was the beginning of a long healing process. My mother and I re-established a mother/son relationship. She and I would eventually develop a friendship that continued until her death, twenty-two years later. The day that she picked me up from juvey was a turning point for her too. She got the opportunity to rekindle the motherhood that she had abandoned that previous year.

I will never know what changed in my mother that day. Why did she all of the sudden take an interest in me?

Three months passed before my mother was able to travel to Portland to visit her two youngest sons. She returned from that visit, more dedicated than ever to bring them back to Ojai. She had part-time employment as a physical therapist's assistant, which meant that there was little financial leniency for additional expenditures. I stayed in school and helped out financially with various part-time jobs, but dishwashing wages fared no better. Together, our meager income provided just enough to cover the monthly rent, bills, and groceries.

However, my mother's suitor at that time offered to provide the funds for bus tickets to liberate Pat and Tim from their deprivation. The image of the two of them when they stepped down from the bus upon their arrival has stayed with me to this day. They looked like prisoners of war. The three of us stayed in that forlorn apartment building on Boardman Rd. with our mother until she decided to move in with the man in her life. Pat and Tim eventually joined her and her husband and stayed in mom's custody for the remainder of their teenage years. This left me as the sole renter of the apartment. The eighty dollars per month fee was threatening at times, but my mediocre paycheck would always find a way to cover my expenses. And I always reserved enough to purchase ingredients for the makings of chicken soup.

I quit using heroin and got clean. Luckily enough, I experienced little to no withdrawal symptoms in the process.

Our father continued to teach and retained his position as a principal in the Clackamas County School District. He and Lynn divorced a few years after my departure from Evergreen Drive. He died in 2010. While at his wake, my brothers and I came upon a picture of him standing behind a podium. We were shocked to find out that in his later years he'd started a foundation to benefit neglected and abused children.

Lynn also became a principal a few years after divorcing my father. To my knowledge, no one kept in touch with her. She passed away in 2020.

Steve joined the services after engaging in several employment opportunities around the valley during 1975. He later married and now has three children.

Pat and Tim both married soon after graduating high school, they had three and two children, respectively. Terry never returned to live in California but remained in Oregon where he and his wife currently live today. They too have three children.

Jules never became a mechanic as far as I know. Shortly after leaving his mother's house, he joined the Navy and stayed in their employment until retirement. I saw him on occasion over the years when he'd come back to visit his mother while on leave.

The beautiful Beatrice, passed away that winter while in Arizona. To this day, I do not think I could have survived that year without her guidance and insight. I still apply her teachings to my life today and think of her often. I also wonder on whose bookshelf sits *The Tao*? Do the eyes that read it now ever wonder about its history?

Bob, the rancher from the orchard, was sadly killed in a car accident the fall after I moved in with my mother. The accident occurred only a mile from the red dam. I will never forget his kindness toward me.

The things that I endured between the ages of thirteen and fourteen gave me the gift of appreciating the things that I have, rather than longing for the things that I don't have. I will never forget the feeling of starvation or the hardness of the surface of the ground that I slept on night after night. These experiences have helped me to appreciate the things that many take for granted on a daily basis. For the last fifty years, beds have always been comfortable and food has always tasted good. I have been so fortunate to experience all that life has given me in the last half-century.

The question of how and why I ended up in the situation that I did remain with me for many years to come. While I have no answer to that question, I have found empathy and compassion for my parents who were human beings with inequities and insecurities of their own. When I think of the past, I frequently recall that stoic old peppercorn tree, rooted deeply in the ground on Mallory Way. It stands as a metaphor for life. For years it endured strong Santa Ana winds and heavy rains, but because of its deep roots and flexible branches, it bent in the wind but did not break. It was firmly attached to the earth, grounded, quite literally. Though it was surrounded by bricks and concrete, its determined root system found the nutrients necessary for its very survival.

I think of my brothers and myself, and how we all started out in life no different than the fallen peppercorns, knocked from the tree by bad weather and scattered into the wind. But no matter how many times a peppercorn is crushed underneath a shoe or car tire, it still has the ability to plant its seed and grow. Trials and tribulations, bad weather, and the winds and rains of life make for more resilient peppercorns and more resilient people. I had always been mesmerized by that grand tree, and now that I have a fuller picture of my life, I can see more clearly why it deserves the honor, respect, and reverence I felt for it in my younger years.

If a meager individual such as myself, no more than a fallen peppercorn, can overcome traumatic events and discover growth and maturity from them, then you too, reader, can overcome hardship and trauma and find empowerment. My story, while sad and dark at times, is meant to be a light in the darkness. I hope that it inspires and encourages those who have faced hardship in the past, or are facing hardship in the present, to persevere in the face of challenge. Never give up hope. Mental strength and fortitude can be grown in times of woe. Life never stays stagnant and the weather is always changing. So ride out the storm little peppercorn, because it just might drop you right where you need to be, into fertile soil that will allow you to germinate. If you stay grounded and sink your roots down deep, you will find the nourishment that you need to flourish and grow.

THE END

About the Author

personal photo

KEVIN MEEHAN is a health care practitioner, re-searcher and developer, owner of an acupuncture and Eastern medicine clinic, and has developed his own healthcare and supplement companies. He relishes the honor and ability to help others heal from a wide range of pathologies. Those that he has been unable to help have inspired him to keep digging, learning, and trying harder to apply himself. Writing to inspire others is his most recent venture. He lives in the community of Jackson, Wyoming and *Fallen Peppercorns* is a memoir and Kevin's second book.